spread love

spread *love*

WORDS OF COMPASSION, PEACE, *and* JOY

MOTHER TERESA

Edited and with commentary by

BRIAN KOLODIEJCHUK, MC

ZONDERVAN®

ZONDERVAN

Spread Love

Copyright © 2024 by Mother Teresa Center

ISBN 978-0-310-16181-3 (HC)
ISBN 978-0-310-16183-7 (audio)
ISBN 978-0-310-16205-6 (ePub)

Library of Congress Cataloging-in-Publication Data is on File.

Published in association with the literary agency of Folio Literary Management, 630 9th Avenue, Suite 1009, New York, NY 10036.

Art direction: Jamie DeBruyn
Cover design: Jamie DeBruyn
Cover image: Getty Images
Interior design: Kristy L. Edwards

Printed in Malaysia

24 25 26 27 28 COS 5 4 3 2 1

FOREWORD

"LIFE IS NOTHING BUT A JOURNEY," MOTHER Teresa tells us. On this journey, some days are daunting; some days are brighter. We all long for a more fulfilling, more meaningful journey. Mother Teresa would not only tell her Sisters but show by her example how to daily quench this longing, this thirst, by clinging to Jesus.

For some time now, it has been on my heart to compile Mother Teresa's encouraging quotes, stories, prayers, and teachings into a short book. The intention was to allow those who are hungry for inspirational thought and spiritual nourishment to take a small pause each day, even amidst a busy schedule, and incorporate a short meditation or a simple prayer into one's daily routine. Mother Teresa's words will give a spiritual flavor to our whole day, and her words of wisdom will help us live a fuller and happier life, closer to the Lord and to those around us.

Throughout this book we are invited to allow Mother Teresa to "walk with us" in the ordinariness of daily life, transforming it into something meaningful, indeed making of it "something beautiful for God," as she loved to say. There are 365 entries, one for each day of the year, offering the opportunity to begin any time of the year to find ample nourishment, consolation, and courage.

Most of the selections here were originally addressed to the members of her religious family, such as Mother Teresa's instructions to her Sisters or to the Contemplative Brothers (originally called the Brothers of the Word); however, these words are applicable to everyone who wishes to deepen their relationship with God, or perhaps just to make a positive difference in their surroundings. Mother Teresa's simple yet profound teachings are rooted in the Word of God. As we read them, meditate on them, and pray with them, they invite us to "put our love into living action," to give concrete form to the Word that has been sown in our hearts.

Mother Teresa's words are easy to understand, as they shed light on the path that leads to greater love, joy, peace, and happiness in our lives. Yet they are also challenging to put into practice, as they urge us to go out of ourselves toward others, especially toward our suffering brothers and sisters, beginning with those who need love at this moment more than we do, those in our own homes and neighborhoods.

During her life Mother Teresa acted as God's messenger, "a carrier of God's love." By her presence, words, and deeds, she pointed out that "God still loves the world through you and through me." Throughout the pages of this book, may she serve as a "spiritual guide" who points us toward the path that the Lord traces for each of us. May her words now be an encouragement to us to bring God's love and compassion to all those we encounter on our way, and so make this world (our own "tiny worlds" especially), a better, nobler, more loving and peaceful place to live, a civilization of love.

Brian Kolodiejchuk, MC

DAY 1

WE SHALL MAKE THIS YEAR A YEAR OF PEACE IN a particular way. To be able to do this we shall try to talk more to God and with God and less with men and to men. Let us preach the peace of Christ like he did. "[He] went about doing good" (Acts 10:38 KJV); he did not stop his works of charity because the Pharisees and others hated him or tried to spoil his Father's work. He just went about doing good. Cardinal Newman wrote, "Help me to spread thy fragrance everywhere I go; let me preach thee without preaching, not by words but by my example by the catching force, the sympathetic influence of what I do, the evident fullness of the love my heart bears to thee."

DAY 2

THE AIM OF A RETREAT IS TO ADVANCE IN THE knowledge and love of God, to purify ourselves, and to reform and transform our lives according to the life of our model, Jesus Christ. It is a time of greater silence, of more fervent prayer, of special penance, and more intense spiritual activity. It is not so much a looking back on the achievements and failure of the past, as a looking forward to a more generous imitation of our Lord himself.

DAY 3

TODAY, WHEN EVERYTHING IS BEING QUESTIONED and changed, let us go back to Nazareth. Jesus had come to redeem the world, to teach us the love of his Father. How strange that he should spend thirty years just doing nothing, wasting his time! Not giving a chance to his personality or to his gifts! We know that at the age of twelve he silenced the learned priests of the temple, who knew so much and so well. But when his parents found him, "he went down . . . to Nazareth, and was subject unto them" (Luke 2:51 KJV). For twenty years we hear no more of him, so that the people were astonished when he went in public to preach. He, a carpenter's son, doing just the humble work in a carpenter's shop for thirty years!

— DAY 4 —

THERE ARE THREE SIGNS OF GENUINE HUMILITY; see if you possess these:

Deference, respect, and obedience toward your superiors.

The joyous acceptance of all humiliations.

Charity toward your sisters, particularly toward those who are poor and humble.

— DAY 5 —

MARY IN THE MYSTERY OF HER ANNUNCIATION and visitation is the very model of the way you should live, because first she received Jesus in her life, then she went in haste to give to her cousin Elizabeth; what she had received, she had to give. You must be like her, giving in haste the Word you have received in meditation. In every Holy Communion, Jesus the Word becomes flesh in our life, a special, delicate, beautiful gift of God; it's a privilege. Why you . . . and not someone else? I don't know. But you must protect it with tender care because he is giving himself, the Word, to you to be made flesh, to each one of you, and to those who will come after.

THE INTERIOR SILENCE IS VERY DIFFICULT, BUT we must make the effort to pray. In silence we will find new energy and true unity. The energy of God will be ours to do all things well, and so will the unity of our thoughts with his thoughts, the unity of our prayers with his prayers, the unity of our actions with his actions, of our life with his life. All our words will be useless unless they come from within. Words that do not give the light of Christ increase the darkness.

DAY 7

PRAYER, TO BE FRUITFUL, MUST COME FROM THE heart and must be able to touch the heart of God. See how Jesus taught his disciples to pray. Call God your Father; praise and glorify his name. Do his will as the saints do it in heaven; ask for daily bread, spiritual and temporal; ask for forgiveness of your own sins and that you may forgive others, and also for the grace not to give in to temptations and for the final grace to be delivered from the evil that is in us and around us.

DAY 8

WE HAVE TO LOVE UNTIL IT HURTS. IT IS NOT enough to say, "I love." We must put that love into a living action. And how do we do that? Give until it hurts. Some time ago, in our children's home, we didn't have sugar for our children. A little boy, four years old, heard "Mother Teresa has no sugar for the children." He went home and told his parents, "I will not eat sugar for three days. I will give my sugar to Mother Teresa." After three days the parents brought him to our house. He was so small that he could scarcely pronounce even my name, and yet he taught me how to love with great love. It was not how much he gave, but that he gave with great love, and he gave until it hurt.

DAY 9

LET THERE BE NO PRIDE NOR VANITY IN THE work. The work is God's work; the poor are God's poor. Work for Jesus and Jesus will work with you, pray with Jesus and Jesus will pray through you. The more you forget yourself, the more Jesus will think of you. The more you detach yourself from self, the more attached Jesus is to you. Put yourself completely under the influence of Jesus so that he may think his thoughts in your mind; do his work through your hands—for you will be all-powerful with him who strengthens you.

DAY 10

WE ARE BUT INSTRUMENTS THAT GOD DEIGNS TO use; these instruments bring forth fruit in the measure that they are united to God, for Saint Paul said, "I have planted, Apollos watered; but God gave the increase" (1 Corinthians 3:6 KJV). We obtain grace in proportion to our sanctity, to our fervor, to our degree of union with our Lord.

DAY 11

OUR OBEDIENCE, BY BEING PROMPT, SIMPLE, BLIND, and cheerful, is the proof of our faith. If "God loves a cheerful giver," how much more would he not love an obedient giver (2 Corinthians 9:7 ESV)? We must obey like

Christ obeyed, unto death, even death on the cross. He saw the will of his Father in everything and everybody, so that he could say, "I always do the things that are pleasing to him" (John 8:29 ESV). He obeyed Caiaphas and Pilate because their authority was given "from above." He submitted to them with obedience and dignity. He did not look at the human limitations of Caiaphas and Pilate. He looked at his Father, for whose love he submitted himself to them. Let us obey like Jesus and our lives will become pleasing to God, and he will say, "This is my beloved child in whom I am well pleased."

— DAY 12 —

WE MUST BE AWARE OF OUR ONENESS WITH Christ, as he was aware of oneness with his Father. Our work is truly apostolic only insofar as we permit him to work in us and through us, with his power, with his desire, and with his love.

—————— DAY 13 ——————

ONE DAY I WAS WALKING DOWN THE STREETS OF
London—and then I saw a man, so huddled up, looking
so lonely, looking so left alone with his head bent down.
So I stopped, I took his hand, I shook his hand, asked him
how he was. And my hand is always very warm, and he
looked up and said, "Oh, after such a long time, I feel the
warmth of a human hand, after such a long time." And his
eyes brightened up, and he sat up. Just that little warmth of
a human hand brought joy into his life. You have to experience
that. You must have your eyes wide open and do it.

—————— DAY 14 ——————

PERFECT PRAYER DOES NOT CONSIST IN MANY
words but in the fervor of the desire that raised the heart
to Jesus. Jesus has chosen us to be souls of prayer. The
value of our actions corresponds exactly to the value of the
prayer we make, and our actions are fruitful only if they
are the true expression of earnest prayer. We must fix our
gaze on Jesus, and if we work together with Jesus, we will

do much better. We get anxious and restless because we try to work alone, without Jesus.

DAY 15

SISTERS, YOUR COMMUNITY MUST BE DEEPLY contemplative, intensely eucharistic, and vibrant with joy. Is your community deeply contemplative, intensely eucharistic, and vibrant with joy? Have that deep silence and oneness with Jesus! Is your mind deeply contemplative, totally surrendered, completely obedient? Have you that deep oneness with Jesus?

DAY 16

"A FAMILY THAT PRAYS TOGETHER STAYS together," said Father Peyton about the family rosary. How much more should this apply to us! Living together, working together, praying together is an aid to piety, a safeguard to chastity, and a mutual advantage in the work for souls. We should not get into the habit of postponing our prayers but make them with the community.

THE POOR ARE VERY BEAUTIFUL PEOPLE. ONE evening we went out and picked up four people from the street. One of them was in a most terrible condition. I told the sisters, "You take care of the other three; I will take care of this one that looks worse." So I did for her all that my love could do. I put her in bed, and there was such a beautiful smile on her face. She took hold of my hand, and she said only "thank you," and she died. I could not help but examine my conscience before her. And I asked, "What would I say if I was in her place?" And my answer was very simple. I would have tried to draw a little attention to myself. I would have said, "I am hungry, I am dying, I am cold, I am in pain," or something. But she gave me much more—she gave me her grateful love. She died with a smile on her face . . . this is the greatness of our people. And that is why we believe what Jesus has said, "I was hungry, I was naked, I was homeless, I was unwanted, unloved, uncared for—and you did it to me" (Matthew 25:35–40 KJV, paraphrased).

DAY 18

DON'T SEARCH FOR JESUS IN FAR LANDS. HE IS not there. He is close to you; he is in you. Just keep the lamp burning and you will always see him. Keep on filling the lamp with all those little drops of love, and you will see how sweet is the Lord you love.

DAY 19

BY FOLLOWING THE VOCATION OF A MISSIONARY of Charity, we stand before the world as ambassadors of peace by preaching the message of love in action that crosses all barriers of nationality, creed, or country. The Indian ambassador in Rome told the people, "These, our sisters, have done more in a short time to bring our two countries closer to each other by their influence of love than we have through official means."

DAY 20

WE WANT SO MUCH TO PRAY PROPERLY AND then we fail. We get discouraged and give up on prayer. God allowed the failure, but he did not want the discouragement. He wants us to be more childlike, more humble, more grateful in prayer, and not to try to pray alone, as we all belong to the mystical body of Christ, which is praying always. There is always prayer; there is no such thing as "I pray," but Jesus in me and Jesus with me prays; therefore, the body of Christ prays.

DAY 21

THESE WORDS OF JESUS, "LOVE ONE ANOTHER; even as I have loved you" (John 13:34 RSV), should be not only a light to us, but they should also be a flame consuming the selfishness that prevents the growth of holiness. Jesus "loved us to the end," to the very limit of love: the cross. This love must come from within, from our union with Christ. It must be an outpouring of our love for God, superior and sisters, a family with the common Father, who is in heaven. Loving must be as normal to us as living and breathing, day after day until our death.

DAY 22

IF YOU ARE PUT IN THE KITCHEN, YOU MUST NOT think it does not require brains—that sitting, standing, coming, going—anything will do. God will not ask that sister how many books she has read, how many miracles she has worked, but he will ask her if she has done her best, for the love of him. Can she in all sincerity say, "I have done my best"? Even if the best is a failure, it must be our best, our utmost.

DAY 23

"I KEEP THE LORD ALWAYS BEFORE ME; BECAUSE he is at my right hand, I shall not be moved," says the psalmist (Psalm 16:8 RSV). God is within me, a more intimate presence than that whereby I am in myself: "In him we live and move and have our being" (Acts 17:28 NRSV). It is he who gives life to all, who gives power and being to all that exists. But for his sustaining presence, all things would cease to be and fall back into nothingness. Consider that you are in God, surrounded and encompassed by God, swimming in God.

DAY 24

JESUS CHRIST HAS TOLD US THAT WE OUGHT "always to pray, and not to faint" (Luke 18:1 KJV), that is, not to grow weary of doing so. Saint Paul said, "Pray without ceasing" (1 Thessalonians 5:17 KJV). God calls all men to this disposition of the heart, of praying always. Let the love of God once take entire and absolute possession of a heart; let it become to that heart like a second nature; let that heart suffer nothing that is contrary to it to enter; let it apply itself continually to increase this love of God by seeking to please him in all things and refusing him nothing that he asks; let it accept as from his hand everything that happens to it; let it have a firm determination never to commit any fault deliberately and knowingly; or if it should fall, to be humble for it and to rise up again at once. Such a heart will pray continually.

DAY 25

AS OUR POOR KEEP GROWING IN POVERTY DUE to the great rise in the cost of living, let us be more careful regarding the poverty in our houses. The daily needs that our poor cannot get, let us be more careful in the use of them, so that we also feel the hardship in food, clothing, water, electricity, and soap—things that our poor often go without. Because we can get these things easily, we use them in abundance, maybe more than we would use if we were at home.

DAY 26

THE KNOWLEDGE WE IMPART MUST BE JESUS crucified, and as Saint Augustine said: "Before allowing his tongue to speak, the apostle ought to raise his thirsting soul to God and then give forth what he has drunk in, and pour forth what he has been filled with"; or as Saint Thomas Aquinas told us: "Those who are called to the works of the active life would be wrong in thinking that their duty dispenses them from the contemplative life. This duty adds to it and does not lessen its necessity."

DAY 27

CONTEMPLATIVE LIFE IS A LIFE OF PRAYER AND penance, and to be in union with God especially through the life of sacrifice. That is why the Church allows the contemplative congregations to grow and to live. Thank God we have all of the contemplatives to help us be really holy. Don't make use of this life as an escape from the world, from the hard work. But grow in that deep intimate union with Jesus and pray for the Church, and for the Society.

DAY 28

FOR US RELIGIOUS, PRAYER IS A SACRED DUTY and sublime mission. Conscious of the many urgent needs and interests we carry in our hands, we will ascend the altar of prayer, take up our rosary, turn to all the other spiritual exercises with great longing, and "go therefore with confidence to the throne of grace: that we may obtain mercy, and find grace in seasonable aid" for ourselves and our souls (Hebrews 4:16 DRA).

DAY 29

A FEW WEEKS AGO I GOT A LETTER FROM A little child from the United States. She was making her first Holy Communion. She told her parents, "Don't worry about special clothes for my First Communion. I will make my First Communion in my school uniform. Don't have any party for me. But please give me the money. I want to send it to Mother Teresa." And yet that little one, just seven or eight years old, already in her heart was loving until it hurt.

DAY 30

THE PRAYER THAT COMES FROM THE MIND AND heart and that we do not read in books is called mental prayer. We must never forget that we are bound by our state to tend toward perfection and to aim ceaselessly at it. The practice of daily mental prayer is necessary to reach our goal. Because it is the breath of life to our soul, holiness is impossible without it. Saint Teresa of Avila said, "She who gives up mental prayer does not require the devil to push her into hell; she goes there of her own accord." It is only by mental prayer and spiritual reading that we can cultivate the gift of prayer. Mental prayer is greatly fostered by simplicity; that is, forgetfulness of self, by mortifications of the body and of our senses, and by frequent aspirations that feed our prayer. "In mental prayer," said Saint John Vianney, "shut your eyes, shut your mouth, and open your heart." In vocal prayer we speak to God; in mental prayer he speaks to us. It is then that God pours himself into us.

 —————— DAY 31 ——————

THE BEST MEANS FOR MAKING SPIRITUAL PRO- gress is prayer and spiritual reading. *Tolle et lege* (take and read), Saint Augustine was told, and after reading, his whole life was changed. So too was that of Saint Ignatius, the wounded soldier, when he read the lives of the saints. How often we ourselves have found the light pouring into our souls during spiritual reading. Saint Thomas à Kempis wrote, "Take then a book into thy hands as Simeon the just man took the child Jesus into his arms; and when you have finished, close the book and give thanks for every word out of the mouth of God, because in the Lord's field you have found a hidden treasure." Saint Bernard said,

"Try not so much to catch the meaning as to relish what you read. Let us not die of starvation in the midst of abundance." There is indeed little advantage in reading if we do not read well. Spiritual reading is one of the most precious spiritual exercises and duties, one that no one can afford to neglect. When choosing a book, never take something above you, but always take one that will give you the greatest spiritual profit.

DAY 32

THE TRUE INTERIOR LIFE MAKES THE ACTIVE life burn forth and consume everything. It makes us find Jesus in the dark holes of the slums, in the most pitiful miseries of the poor, as the God-man naked on the cross, mournful, despised by all, the man of suffering, crushed like a worm by the scourging and the crucifixion. It makes us serve Jesus in the poor.

—————— DAY 33 ——————

CONFESSION MAKES THE SOUL STRONG BECAUSE a really good confession—the confession of a child in sin coming back to her Father—always begets humility, and humility is strength. We may go to confession as often as we want and to whom we want, but we are not encouraged to seek spiritual direction from any and every source. The confessional is not a place for useless conversation or gossip. The topic should be my sins, my sorrow, my forgiveness: how to overcome my temptations, how to practice virtue, how to increase in the love of God.

—————— DAY 34 ——————

THE TOUCH MAY CARRY DIVINE LOVE OR destruction. When in touching we seek Christ, we touch the suffering body of Christ, and this touch will make us heroic; it will make us forget the repugnance and the natural tendencies in us. It will put into our touch the healing power of love. . . . We need the eyes of deep faith to see Christ in the broken body and dirty clothes under which the most beautiful one among the sons of men hides.

We shall need the hands of Christ to touch these bodies wounded by pain and suffering.

—————————————— DAY 35 ——————————————

YOU NEED ONLY ASK AT NIGHT BEFORE YOU GO to bed, "What did I do to Jesus today? What did I do for Jesus today? What did I do with Jesus today?" You have only to look at your hands. This is the best examination of conscience.

—————————————— DAY 36 ——————————————

AND HOW WILL YOU FIND JESUS? HE HAS MADE it so easy for us. "Love one another; even as I have loved you" (John 13:34 RSV). And if we have gone astray, there is the beautiful sacrament of confession. We go to confession a sinner full of sin. We come from confession a sinner without sin by the greatness of the mercy of God. No need for us to despair. No need for us to commit suicide. No need for us to be discouraged—no need, if we have understood the tenderness of God's love. You are precious to him. He loves you, and he loves you so tenderly that he has carved you on the palm of his hand. These are God's words written in the Scripture (Isaiah 49:16, paraphrased). You know them. Remember them when your heart feels restless, when your heart feels hurt, when your heart feels like breaking everything—remember, "I am precious to him. He loves me. He has called me by my name. I am his. He loves me. God loves me" (Isaiah 43:4, paraphrased). And to prove that love, he died on the cross.

DAY 37

ONE EVENING A GENTLEMAN CAME TO OUR house and he told me, "There is a Hindu family with eight children, and they have not eaten for a long time. Do something for them." And I took some rice, and I went straight to them. I could see in the children's faces terrible hunger. And yet the mother took the rice, she divided it into two portions, and she went out. When she came back, I asked her, "Where did you go? What did you do?" And she gave me one answer only: "They are hungry also." She had next-door neighbors, a Muslim family, and she knew they were hungry. I did not bring any more rice for that day because I wanted them to experience the joy of giving. I was not surprised that she gave, but I was surprised that she knew that they were hungry. Do we know? Do we have time to know? Do we have time to smile at somebody?

DAY 38

HE TAUGHT US TO LEARN FROM HIM, TO BE MEEK and humble of heart. If we are meek and humble, we will love each other as he loves us. That is why we should ask again and again that we bring prayer back into our families. The family that prays together stays together. And to stay together you will love one another as God loves you, and he loves you tenderly.

DAY 39

I NEVER FORGOT THE OPPORTUNITY I HAD IN visiting a home where they had all these old parents of sons and daughters who had just put them in an institution and forgotten them. I went there, and I saw in that home they had everything, beautiful things, but everybody was looking toward the door. And I did not see a single one with a smile on their face. And I turned to the sister and I said, "How is that? How is it that these people who have everything here, why are they all looking toward the door? Why are they not smiling?"

I am so used to seeing smiles on our people; even the dying ones smile. She said, "This happens nearly every day. They are expecting, they are hoping that a son or a daughter will come to visit them." They are hurt because they are forgotten. And see—this is where love comes. That poverty comes right into our own home, we even neglect to love. Maybe in our own family we have somebody who is feeling lonely, who is feeling sick, who is feeling worried, and these are difficult days for everybody. Are we there? Are we there to receive them?

—————— DAY 40 ——————

HOW BEAUTIFUL IT IS TO SEE THE LOVE FOR each other a living reality! Young sisters, have deep love and respect for your older sisters. Older sisters, treat your younger sisters with respect and love, for they, like you, belong to Jesus. He has chosen each one of you for himself, to be his love and his light in the world. The simplest way of becoming his light is by being kind and loving, thoughtful, and sincere with each other: "By this shall all [people] know that you are my disciples, if you have love one for another" (John 13:35 DRA).

—————————— DAY 41 ——————————

THESE TWO LIVES, ACTION AND CONTEMPLATION, instead of excluding each other, call for each other's help, implement and complete each other. Action, to be productive, has need of contemplation. The latter, when it gets to a certain degree of intensity, diffuses some of its excess on the first. By contemplation the soul draws directly from the heart of God the graces that the active life must distribute.

—————————— DAY 42 ——————————

I WAS SURPRISED IN THE WEST TO SEE SO MANY young boys and girls given to drugs, and I tried to find out why. Why is it like that when those in the West have so many more things than those in the East? And the answer was "because there is no one in the family to receive them." Our children depend on us for everything—their security, their coming to know and love God. For all of this, they look to us with trust, hope, and expectation. Father and mother are so busy they have no time. The child goes back out on the street and gets involved in something. We are talking of loving the child, which is where love and peace must begin.

DAY 43

IN WORKING FOR THE SALVATION OF OTHERS, WE secure our own, because it is so pleasing to God that it will merit for us great graces. It affords opportunities for acquiring many virtues, especially charity, patience, self-denial, humility. It was for this that our Lord came down to earth. Our lives, or rather our work, is so closely resembling that of our Lord that we should never cease blessing God for his goodness to us in calling us to this Society.

DAY 44

IN AUSTRALIA, WHERE OUR SISTERS ARE WORK-
ing, we go to the houses of the poor and wash and clean
and do all kinds of things there. Then I went to one man's
house, and I asked him, "May I clean your house?" And
he said, "I'm all right." I said, "You'll be more all right if
you let me do it." So he allowed me to clean his place. And
then I saw in the corner of his room a big lamp full of dirt.
I asked him, "Don't you light this lamp?" He said, "For
whom? For years nobody has come to me—for years." So I
said, "Will you light the lamp if the sisters come?" He said,
"Yes." So I cleaned the lamp. The sisters started going to
his house, to his place, and the lamp was lit. I completely
forgot about him. After two years I got news from him
saying, "Tell my friend the light she has lit in my life is
still burning."

DAY 45

WE NEED TO AVOID PRIDE. PRIDE DESTROYS
everything. That's why Jesus told his disciples to be
meek and humble. He didn't say contemplation is a big

thing—but being meek and humble with one another. If you understand that, you understand your vocation. To live his way is the key to being meek and humble.

DAY 46

LET US ASK OUR LADY TO BE WITH US. LET US ask her to give us her heart so beautiful, so pure, so immaculate—her heart so full of love and humility that we may be able to receive Jesus as the Bread of Life, that we may love him as she loved him and serve him in the distressing disguise of the poor.

DAY 47

A SISTER WAS TELLING ME THAT JUST TWO OR three weeks ago she and some other sisters picked up a man from the streets in Bombay and brought him home. We have a big place donated to us that we have turned into a home for the dying. This man was brought there and the sisters took care of him. They loved him and treated him with dignity. Right away they discovered that the whole of his back had no skin, no flesh. It was all eaten up. After they washed him, they put him on his bed, and this sister told me that she had never seen so much joy as she saw on the face of that man. Then I asked her, "What did you feel when you were removing those worms from his body; what did you feel?" And she looked at me and said, "I've never felt the presence of Christ so clearly; I've never really believed the word of Jesus saying, 'I was sick and you did it to me.' But his presence was there and I could see it on that man's face." This is the gift of God.

DAY 48

WE ARE AT HIS DISPOSAL. HE WANTS YOU TO BE sick in bed, all right. He wants you to be in the street, all right. He wants you to be cooking, all right. He wants you to clean the toilets, all right. All right. Everything is all right. We must say, "I belong to you. You can do whatever you like." And this . . . is our strength and this is the joy of the Lord.

DAY 49

WE ARE THE SERVANTS OF THE POOR. WE GIVE wholehearted, free service to the poor. In the world the people are paid for their work. We are paid by God. We are bound by a vow to love and serve the poor, and to live as the poor with the poor.

DAY 50

THIS WILL NEED MUCH SACRIFICE, BUT IF WE really mean to pray and want to pray, we must be ready to do it now. These are only the first steps toward prayer, but if we never make the first step with determination, we will not reach the last one: the presence of God.

DAY 51

A FEW WEEKS AGO TWO YOUNG PEOPLE CAME to our house, and they gave me lots of money to feed the people. I said to them, "Where did you get so much money?" They said, "Two days ago we got married. Before our wedding we decided we will not buy wedding clothes, we will not have a wedding feast, and we will give you the money." I know what that means for a Hindu family, and how big a sacrifice they had made. Then I asked them, "But why did you do it?" And they said, "We love each other so much that we wanted to share the joy of loving with the people you serve." And we experienced the joy of loving. And where does this love begin? At home. And how does it begin? By sharing until it hurts, by loving until it hurts.

DAY 52

GOD WANTS US TO BE CLOSE TO HIM. SAINT JOHN says that he opened his heart. Become small and then you will be able to enter it. It is one thing for me to say I am a sinner, but let someone else say that about me and then I feel it; I am up in arms. If I am falsely accused, I may suffer, but deep down there is joy, whereas if the correction be founded on even a small reality—something in me having deserved it—then often it hurts more. We must be happy that our faults are known as they are and be open with the superiors about faults and shortcomings.

ONE DAY IN CALCUTTA A MAN CAME WITH A PRE-scription and said, "My only child is dying and this medicine can be brought only from outside of India." Just at that time, while we were still talking, a man came with a basket of medicine. Right on the top of that basket, there was this medicine. If it had been inside, I would not have seen it. If he had come before, or if he had come afterward, I could not have seen it. But just at that time, out of the millions and millions of children in the world, God in his tenderness was concerned with this little child of the slums of Calcutta enough to send, just at that time, that amount of medicine to save that child. That is the tenderness and the love of God, because every little one, in a poor family or a rich family, is a child of God, created for greater things.

THE MORE REPUGNANT THE WORK, THE GREATER should be our faith and cheerful devotion. That we feel the repugnance is but natural, but when we overcome it for love of Jesus, we may become heroic. Very often it has happened in the lives of the saints that a heroic overcoming of something repugnant has been the lift to a high sanctity. Such was the case of Saint Francis of Assisi, who when meeting a leper completely disfigured, drew back, but then overcoming himself, kissed the terrible disfigured face. The result was that Francis was filled with an untold joy. He became the complete master of himself, and the leper walked away praising God for his cure.

 ———— DAY 55 ————

DO WE TREAT THE POOR AS OUR DUSTBINS TO give whatever we cannot use or eat? I cannot eat this food so I give it to the poor. I cannot use this thing or that piece of cloth so I give it to the poor. Am I then sharing the poverty of the poor? Do I identify myself with the poor I serve? Am I one with them? Do I share with them as Jesus shared with me?

WE DO NOT ALLOW OURSELVES TO BE DISHEART-
ened by any failure as long as we have done our best,
neither do we glory in our success but refer all to God in
deepest thankfulness. Humanly speaking, if a sister fails
in her work, we are inclined to attribute it to all kinds of
human weaknesses—she has no brains, she did not do her
best, and so on. Yet in the eyes of God she is not a failure
if it is her best. She is his coworker still.

WE MUST NEVER THINK ANY ONE OF US IS INDIS-
pensable. God has ways and means—he may allow
everything to go upside down in the hands of a talented
and capable sister. God sees only her love. You may be
exhausted with work, even kill yourself, but unless your
work is interwoven with love, it is useless. God does not
need our work.

—— DAY 58 ——

AS WE ARE AND MEAN TO REMAIN POOR WITH the poor for the love of Christ, we willingly offer up the pleasure of our own room. The common dormitory is a means of practicing many virtues; poverty, modesty, cleanliness, and tidiness. It also helps to foster the family spirit.

—— DAY 59 ——

TOTAL SURRENDER TO GOD MUST COME IN SMALL details just as it comes in big details. It's nothing but that single phrase, "Yes, I accept whatever you give, and I give whatever you take." And this is just a simple duty for us to be holy. We must not create difficulties in our own mind. To be holy doesn't mean to do extraordinary things, to understand big things, but it is a simple acceptance, because I have given myself to God, because I belong to him—my total surrender. He could put me here. He could put me there. He can use me. He can *not* use me. It doesn't matter because I belong so totally to him that it can be just what he wants to do with me.

HUMILITY IS NOTHING BUT TRUTH. "WHAT DO you have that you did not receive?" asks Saint Paul (1 Corinthians 4:7 ESV). If I have received everything, what good have I of my own? If we are convinced of this, we will never raise our head in pride. If you are humble, nothing will touch you, neither praise nor disgrace, because you know what you are. If you are blamed, you will not be discouraged; if they call you a saint, you will not put yourself on a pedestal. If you are a saint, thank God. If you are a sinner, do not remain so.

---- DAY 61 ----

THE CONTEMPLATIVE AND APOSTOLIC FRUITFUL- ness of our way of life depends on our being rooted in Christ Jesus our Lord by our deliberate choice of small and simple means for the fulfillment of our mission and by our fidelity to humble work of love among the spiritually poorest, identifying ourselves with them, sharing their poverty and insecurities until it hurts.

DAY 62

WE NEED TO BE PURE IN HEART TO SEE JESUS IN the person of the spiritually poorest. Therefore, the more disfigured the image of God is in that person, the greater will be our faith and devotion in seeking Jesus' face and lovingly ministering to him. We consider it an honor to serve Christ in the distressing disguise of the spiritually poorest; we do it with deep gratitude and reverence in a spirit of fraternal sharing.

DAY 63

IF WE REALLY WANT TO GROW IN HOLINESS, OBE-dience is the sure way. Let us turn constantly to our Lady to teach us how to obey, to Jesus who was obedient unto death: he, being God, "went down with them, and came to Nazareth, and was subject unto them: but his mother kept all these sayings in her heart" (Luke 2:51 KJV).

DAY 64

ONE THING IS NECESSARY FOR US—CONFESSION. Confession is nothing but humility in action. We called it penance, but really it is a sacrament of love, a sacrament of forgiveness. That is why confession should not be a place in which to talk for long hours about our difficulties. It is a place where I allow Jesus to take away from me everything that divides, that destroys. When there is a gap between me and Christ, when my love is divided, anything can come to fill the gap. We should be very simple and childlike in confession. "Here I am as a child going to her Father." If a child is not yet spoiled and has not learned to tell lies, he will tell everything. This is what I mean by being childlike. Confession is a beautiful act of great love. Only in confession can we go as sinners with sin and come out as sinners without sin.

DAY 65

IF WE EARNESTLY DESIRE HOLINESS, SELF-DENIAL must enter our lives fully after prayer. The easiest form of self-denial is control over our bodily senses. We must practice interior mortification and bodily penances also. How generous are we with God in our mortifications?

DAY 66

LENT IS A TIME WHEN WE RELIVE THE PASSION of Christ. Let it not be just a time when our feelings are roused, but let it be a change that comes through cooperation with God's grace in real sacrifice of self. Sacrifice, to be real, must cost; it must hurt; it must empty us of self. Let us go through the Passion of Christ day by day.

DAY 67

WHEN WE RECOLLECT THAT IN THE MORNING we have held within our hands an all-holy God, we are more ready to abstain from whatever could soil their purity. Hence deep reverence for our own person; reverence for others, treating all with accepted marks of courtesy, but abstaining from sentimental feelings or ill-ordered affections.

—————— DAY 68 ——————

RIGHT FROM THE VERY BEGINNING, LEARN TO obey. For obedience is a way straight to God. You don't have to write with crooked lines. There is a very straight way to the heart of Jesus. You will never, never, never, never, never go astray, never make a mistake, if you understand obedience. The superior who tells you to do this or do that may make a mistake. I may make a mistake in telling the sisters do this and go here and go there. I may make a mistake but that sister who does what I tell her is infallible. I may make a big mistake but that sister is infallible. So the same thing, you brothers. This conviction is total surrender.

—————— DAY 69 ——————

THAT IS WHAT JESUS DID, NO? WHEN HE BECAME man, that is his total surrender to his Father; that is why again and again we hear the word *Father* in most all his days; even when he was preaching, when he was teaching, when he was with the people, continually he taught the word *Father*. "I have come to do the will of my Father." "I have been sent by the Father." "I and my Father are one" (John 10:30 KJV). "I love you just as the Father loves me" (John 15:9 GNT). All the time the Father is involved. He belonged so much to the Father that there was no separation, there was no division. There was no doubt. There was no question at all. And this is what a brother of the Word has to be: complete oneness with Christ, complete oneness with the Word of God. And that Word of God that you receive in prayer, in adoration, in contemplation, in that aloneness with God, that same Word you have to give to others.

—————— DAY 70 ——————

OUR VOCATION IS TO BELONG TO JESUS. THE EAS-iest way and the simplest way of belonging—we must have a reason for belonging—is this: the spirit that makes us do that giving of self is that total surrender to God, without any reserve, without any counting the cost, without examining. We call that in other words *blind obedience* and *blind surrender*. It is like our Lady: after she knew the will of God, she said yes. And she never withdrew that yes. It was one continual yes in her life. It is the same thing for us. . . . The whole of our life must come to that one word *yes*. Yes to God: that is holiness, that we allow God to take from us whatever he wants and to give whatever he wants and that we accept whatever he gives with joy, and that we give whatever he takes with joy. That is yes in action.

—————— DAY 71 ——————

FREQUENT RECEPTION OF THE HOLY EUCHARIST is the wheat of the elect. The reason is that we are thus intimately united to God, and Holy Communion is a symbol of this blessed union. Besides, the Blessed Sacrament detaches us from the love of creatures, in which lies great danger to chastity. Among the effects of Holy Communion are to be reckoned the lessening of concupiscence and the increase of charity. Therefore, a frequent, fervent, loving reception of the Blessed Sacrament with great purity of soul will protect this virtue.

DAY 72

BY THE VOW OF POVERTY WE DEPRIVE OUR-
selves of the possession and free use of temporal goods.
Its virtue causes the destruction of inordinate attachment
to the things of this world. The vow is the means and the
virtue is the end. The principal means of observing the
essentials of poverty is the strict observance of the common life; that is, everyone, including the superior, should
be satisfied with the food, clothing, and outfit given to all
alike without the least privilege for any expense but what
is truly necessary.

DAY 73

IT IS DIFFICULT TO PRAY IF YOU DON'T KNOW
how to pray, but we must help ourselves to pray. The first
means to use is silence. Souls of prayer are souls of great
silence. We cannot put ourselves directly in the presence
of God if we do not practice internal and external silence.
Therefore, we shall take as a special point silence of mind,
eyes, and tongue.

—————— DAY 74 ——————

AND THEN WE LOOK AT THE TABERNACLE, AND I
see how much Jesus loves me now. Do I know that? Is my
heart so clean that I can see Jesus there? And to make it
easy for you and for me to see Jesus, he made himself the
Bread of Life, so that we can receive life, that we may have
life, life of love, life of peace, life of joy. Find Jesus, and you
will find peace.

—————— DAY 75 ——————

DURING LENT WE SHALL IN A SPECIAL WAY AND
with deep feeling meditate on the Passion of our Lord and
examine our conscience on what sin of ours caused that
special pain to Jesus. . . . I will make reparation and share
that pain. . . . I shall keep strict custody of my eyes; I shall
keep clean thoughts in my mind; I shall touch the sick with
greater gentleness and compassion; I shall keep the silence of
the heart with greater care, so that in the silence of my heart
I hear his words of comfort, and from the fullness of my
heart I comfort Jesus in the distressing disguise of the poor.
I shall confess especially my neglect of penance.

DAY 76

TO BE ABLE TO LOVE CHRIST WITH UNDIVIDED love in chastity through the freedom of poverty, in the total surrender of obedience and wholehearted free service to the poorest of the poor and others as Christ loves you and me, while we await his coming in glory: this is the whole rule of life of [a Missionary of Charity]. Let Jesus use you without consulting you, and you will be holy because you belong to him.

DAY 77

DURING THIS LENT LET US IMPROVE OUR SPIRIT of prayer and recollection. Let us free our minds from all that is not Jesus. If you find it difficult to pray, ask him again and again, "Jesus, come into my heart, pray in me and with me, that I may learn from thee how to pray." If you pray more, you will pray better. Take the help of all your senses to pray.

DAY 78

THE FIRST STEP TO BECOMING HOLY IS TO WILL it. Saint Thomas said, "Sanctity consists in nothing else than a firm resolve, the heroic act of a soul abandoning herself to God. By an upright will we love God, we choose God, we run toward God, we reach him, we possess him. O good, good will which transforms me into the image of God and makes me like him!"

DAY 79

YOU MUST ALLOW THE FATHER TO BE A GAR-dener, to prune. You will be pruned, don't worry. He has his own way of pruning you. You must allow him to do it. See if you go to Tor Fiscale, the way they have pruned the vine there, my goodness. . . . I was looking at it and I wondered, "How can leaves or branches or fruit come on this thing?" But a man who knows well about vines pruned it, and he has pruned it right up to the ends of the stems. How branches will come, how leaves will come, how the fruit will come, I don't know. But quite possibly if I come here after two months I will see it all covered with grapes because of the pruning. It is the same for you. Now you are being pruned well, cut off completely, and you don't see anything—no leaves, no branches, nothing.

DAY 80

JOY IS ONE OF THE BEST SAFEGUARDS AGAINST temptation. The devil is a carrier of dust and dirt; he uses every chance to throw what he has at us. A joyful heart knows how to protect herself from such dirt. Jesus can take full possession of our soul only if it surrenders itself joyfully. "A saint who is sad is a sad saint," Saint Francis de Sales used to say. Saint Teresa was worried about her sisters only when she saw any of them lose their joy.

DAY 81

AS JESUS CAN NO LONGER LIVE HIS PASSION IN his body, Mother Church gives the opportunity to allow Jesus to live his Passion and death in our body, heart, and soul. Though there is no comparison with his Passion, still we need so much grace just to accept whatever he gives and give whatever he takes with joy, love, and a smile.

DAY 82

JESUS IS GOING TO DO GREAT THINGS WITH YOU brothers if you let him do it and if you don't try to interfere with him. We interfere with God's plans when we push in someone or something else not suitable for us. Be very strict with yourself, and then be very strict with what you are receiving from outside. People may come with wonderful ideas, with beautiful things, but anything that takes you away from the reality of what you have given to God must remain outside.

DAY 83

LET US OFTEN SAY DURING THE DAY, "WASH AWAY my sins and cleanse me from all my iniquity." How it must hurt Jesus dwelling in our heart to feel in our hearts this bitterness, this hurt, this revengeful feeling made of jealousy and pride! My children, let us be sincere and ask to be forgiven. Is my love for the other members of the community so great, so real as to forgive, not out of duty but out of love?

— DAY 84 —

TRY TO INCREASE YOUR LOVE FOR THE HOLY Mass and the Passion of Christ by accepting with joy all the little sacrifices that come daily. Do not pass by the small gifts, for they are very precious for yourself and for others.

— DAY 85 —

WHEN OUR LORD WANTED SISTERS FOR HIS work among the poor, he expressly asked for the poverty of the cross. Our Lord on the cross possessed nothing. He was on the cross, which was given by Pilate. The nails and the crown were given by the soldiers. He was naked when he died; cross, nails, and crown were taken away from him and he was wrapped in a shroud given by a kind heart and buried in a tomb that was not his. Yet Jesus need not have done all this. He could have died as a king, and he could have risen from the dead as a king. He chose poverty because he knew in his infinite knowledge and wisdom that it is the real means of possessing God, of conquering his heart, of bringing his love down to this earth.

———————— DAY 86 ————————

IN HIS PASSION, JESUS TAUGHT US HOW TO FORgive out of love, how to forget out of humility. So let us at the beginning of the Passion of Christ examine our hearts fully and see if there is any unforgiven hurt, unforgotten bitterness.

———————— DAY 87 ————————

EVEN IN HIS PASSION OUR LORD SAID, "THY WILL be done, which means, do with me what you want." And that was the hardest thing for our Lord in the last moment. That is why they say that the Passion in Gethsemane was much greater than even the crucifixion, because it was his heart, his soul that was being crucified, while on the cross it was his body that was crucified. That's why on the cross he never said, "Thy will be done." He accepted in silence, and he gave his mother, and he said "I thirst" and "It is finished." But nowhere, not once did he say, "Thy will be done," because he had already totally accepted the Father's will during that terrible struggle of the desolation and the loneliness. And the only way that we know that that hour was so difficult for him was when he told the apostles: "Could you not stay one hour with me?" He needed consolation.

———— DAY 88 ————

IT MUST HAVE BEEN SO HARD TO HAVE BEEN scourged, to have been spat upon. "Take it away," Jesus prayed during his agony. His Father didn't come to him directly and say, "This is my beloved Son," but he consoled him through a creature, an angel. Let us pray that we fill our hearts with Jesus' surrender, that we understand total surrender.

---------- **DAY 89** ----------

DO YOU UNDERSTAND, BROTHERS? SUFFERING, pain, humiliation—this is the kiss of Jesus. At times you come so close to Jesus on the cross that he can kiss you. I once told this to a lady who was suffering very much. She answered, "Tell Jesus not to kiss me, to stop kissing me." That suffering has to come that came in the life of our Lady, that came in the life of Jesus—it has to come in our life also. Only never put on a long face. Suffering is a gift from God. It is between you and Jesus alone.

---------- **DAY 90** ----------

LOVING TRUST IS ONLY THE FRUIT OF TOTAL SUR- render. You cannot have trust unless you are one with a person. Total surrender and loving trust are twins. The greatest suffering of Christ was his loneliness—more suffering than the crucifixion. He said "My Father"—three times—"Take away the chalice." Jesus could trust his Father like that because he knew him. A sister cannot trust you and you [cannot] trust her unless you know each other, unless there is some communication, some kind of oneness.

DAY 91

WE OFTEN PRAY, "LET ME SHARE WITH YOU YOUR pain; I want to be the spouse of Jesus crucified," and yet when a little spittle of an uncharitable remark or a stroke of pain or a thorn of thoughtlessness is given to us, how we forget that this is the time to share with him his shame and pain.

DAY 92

IT IS VERY DIFFICULT TO UNDERSTAND WHAT the connection is between our penances and the Passion of Christ. Saint Paul said, "I fulfill what is wanting in the Passion of Christ" (Colossians 1:24, paraphrase). We must constantly follow in the footsteps of Jesus Christ and in a certain manner crucify our own flesh. Our suffering will never come to that degree reached by the saints and martyrs.

———— DAY 93 ————

I THINK THAT THE PASSION OF CHRIST IS A wonderful way for us to learn how to love one another, especially when we are hurt or resent obedience through grumbling or we are blamed for something. Jesus didn't ask why we hurt him with the crown of thorns—this is where we learn the "silence of love." . . . Let us not resent but have the humility to accept the cross without pride. Maybe we can't hurt back so we withdraw. We don't want to smile or talk, but avoid. Jesus didn't avoid. In Gethsemane, Jesus just walked between them and said, "I am Jesus of Nazareth" (John 18:6, paraphrase). The Passion of Jesus is one more great lesson of his tender love for us, showing us how to love one another.

———— DAY 94 ————

SUFFERING HAS TO COME BECAUSE IF YOU LOOK at the cross, he has got his head bending down. He wants to kiss you, and he has both hands open wide. He wants to embrace you. He has his heart opened wide to receive you.

Then when you feel miserable inside, look at the cross and you will know what is happening. Suffering, pain, sorrow, humiliation, feelings of loneliness are nothing but the kiss of Jesus, a sign that you have come so close that he can kiss you.

<hr />

DAY 95

"[JESUS HAS] CALLED THEE BY THY NAME; THOU art mine" (Isaiah 43:1 KJV). "You are precious to me—I love you." If he is like that with me, he must be like that with my sister, my brother also. She too has been called and is the spouse of Jesus Christ. . . . For me, the way I understand it, those words, "I belong to him," mean that even if I sin—he accepts me as I am. Then why do I keep that grudge against my sister [my brother] in my heart? If I have not forgiven my sister, my brother, then I have not understood his love for me. Look at the cross and see where you are. Jesus need not have died like that, need not have been born and to go through that agony in Gethsemane.

DAY 96

EASTER IS ONE OF THE FEASTS OF OUR SOCIETY, a feast of joy, the joy of the Lord. Let nothing so disturb us, so fill us with sorrow or discouragement, as to make us forget the joy of the resurrection.

DAY 97

MAY THE JOY OF OUR RISEN LORD BE YOUR strength in your work, your way to the Father, your light to guide you, and your bread of life.

DAY 98

SEE THE COMPASSION OF CHRIST TOWARD JUDAS, the man who received so much love, and yet he betrayed his own Master, the Master who kept the sacred silence and would not betray him to his companions. Jesus could have easily spoken in public, as some of you do, and told the hidden intentions and deeds of Judas to the others, but he did not do so. He rather showed mercy and charity; instead of condemning him, he called him a friend. If Judas had only looked into the eyes of Jesus like Peter did, today Judas would have been the fruit of God's mercy. Jesus always had compassion.

DAY 99

FIRST, CONFESSION; AFTER IT, ASK FOR SPIRITUAL direction if necessary. The reality of my sins must come first. For most of us there is the danger of forgetting that we are sinners and must go to confession as sinners. We must want the precious blood to wash away our sins. We must go to God to tell him we are sorry for all we have done that may have hurt him.

DAY 100

PENANCE IS NOT ONLY HOW MUCH, BUT HOW much *love* you put in it. It is because we see the suffering of Jesus outside, we need the spirit of sacrifice. We can share in people's suffering only if we do it. It's a conviction, not because you have been told. We have to be told, but that conviction must come from inside, even if nobody does it.

DAY 101

AGAIN AND AGAIN WE HEAR THAT SENTENCE, "Unless you become like a little child, you cannot enter into heaven" (Matthew 18:3, paraphrased). And what is this being a little child? It is having a clean heart, a pure heart, a heart that holds Jesus, a heart that can say again and again, "Jesus in my heart. I believe in your tender love for me. I love you." This is the heart that you, and I, even the youngest in this place must be able to look up, to look up at the cross and understand how much Jesus loved me, each one separately.

DAY 102

WHAT IS DEPENDENCE ON DIVINE PROVIDENCE? A firm and lively faith that God can and will help us. That he can is evident because he is almighty. That he will is certain because he promised it in so many passages of Holy

Scripture and because he is infinitely faithful to all his promises. Christ encourages us to this lively confidence in these words: "Therefore I tell you, whatever you ask in prayer, believe that you have received it, and it will be yours" (Mark 11:24 RSV).

Therefore, the apostle Peter also commanded us to throw all cares upon the Lord, who provides for us. And why should God not care for us since he sent us his Son and, with him, all?

---DAY 103---

SELF-KNOWLEDGE IS VERY NECESSARY FOR CONfession. That is why the saints could say they were wicked criminals. They saw God and then saw themselves, and they saw the difference. Hence they were not surprised when anyone accused them, even falsely. They knew themselves and knew God. We take hurt because we do not know ourselves, and our eyes are not fixed on God alone; so we do not have real knowledge of God. When the saints looked upon themselves with such horror, they really meant it. They were not pretending.

KNOWLEDGE WILL MAKE YOU STRONG AS DEATH.
Love Jesus generously. Love him trustfully, without looking back and without fear. Give yourself fully to Jesus. He
will use you to accomplish great things on the condition
that you believe much more in his love than in your weakness. Believe in him. Trust in him with blind and absolute
confidence because he is Jesus. Believe that Jesus and Jesus
alone is life, and sanctity is nothing but that same Jesus
intimately living in you; only then his hand will be free
with you. Give yourself unswervingly, conforming yourself
in all things to his holy will, which is made known to you
through your superior.

—————DAY 105—————

REMEMBER THAT THE PASSION OF CHRIST ENDS
always in the joy of the resurrection of Christ, so when you
feel in your own heart the suffering of Christ, remember
the resurrection has to come, the joy of Easter has to dawn.

Never let anything so fill you with sorrow as to make you forget the joy of Christ risen.

—DAY 106—

TRUST IN THE GOOD GOD WHO LOVES US, WHO cares for us, who sees all, knows all, can do all things for my good and the good of souls. One thing Jesus asks of me: that I lean upon him; that in him alone I put complete trust; that I surrender myself to him unreservedly. I need to give up my own desires in the work of my perfection. Even when all goes wrong, and I feel as if I were a ship without a compass, I must give myself completely to him.

—DAY 107—

MAY THE JOY AND LOVE OF THE RISEN JESUS BE always with you, in you, and among you, so that we all become the true witnesses of his Father's love for the world: "For God loved the world so much that he gave his Son" (John 3:16, paraphrased). Let us also love God so much that we give ourselves to him in each other and in his poor.

—DAY 108—

AM I CONVINCED OF CHRIST'S LOVE FOR ME AND mine for him? This conviction is like sunlight, which makes the sap of life rise and the buds of sanctity bloom. This conviction is the rock on which sanctity is built. What must we do to get this conviction? We must know Jesus, love Jesus, serve Jesus. We know him through prayers, meditations, and spiritual duties. We love him through holy Mass and the sacraments and through that intimate union of love.

—DAY 109—

WHAT IS OUR SPIRITUAL LIFE? A LOVE UNION with Jesus—the divine and the human give themselves completely to one another. All that Jesus asks of me is to give myself to him in all poverty and nothingness.

—————— DAY 110 ——————

"I WILL BE A SAINT" MEANS I WILL DESPOIL myself of all that is not God. I will strip my heart and empty it of all created things; I will live in poverty and detachment. I will renounce my will, my inclinations, my whims and fancies, and make myself a willing slave to the will of God. Yes, my children, this is what I pray for daily—for each one—that we each may become a slave to the will of God.

—————— DAY 111 ——————

THE CHURCH EXPECTS CONGREGATIONS TO GIVE saints—expects our Society to give saints. Can each one of us look up and say, "Yes—as far as it was in my power, I, whom God can use to the full, have been used to the full." *Saints* in our Society means "total surrender, loving trust, cheerfulness." Are we giving that to the Church? The whole Society together, communities together, individuals together? No one can answer this for you.

DAY 112

OFTEN UNDER THE PRETEXT OF HUMILITY, OF confidence, of abandonment, have we not forgotten the use of our strong will? We must have a real living resolution to reach holiness. Saint Teresa says that Satan is terribly afraid of resolute souls—everything depends on these two phrases: *I will* or *I will not*. Into this "I will," I must put all my energy. . . . What is a saint but a resolute soul—a soul that uses power plus action.

DAY 113

OUR IDEAL IS NO ONE BUT JESUS. WE MUST THINK as he thinks, love as he loves, wish as he wishes; we must permit him to use us to the full. It is beautiful to see the humility of Christ. Who being in the form of God thought it not robbery to be equal with God, "but emptied himself, taking the form of a servant, being made in the likeness of men, and in habit found as a man" (Philippians 2:7–8 DRA).

TO CHILDREN AND TO THE POOR, TO ALL THOSE who suffer and are lonely, give them always a happy smile; give them not only your care but also your heart. We may not be able to give much but we can always give the joy that springs from a heart that is in love with God. Joy is very infectious. Therefore, be always full of joy when you go among the poor.

INTENSE LOVE DOES NOT MEASURE; IT JUST gives. To be an apostle of the Sacred Heart, one must be burning with love, intense love for the sisters, which does not measure. It gives. If you want peace, you cannot just say anything you please, the first word that comes into your head.

─────── DAY 116 ───────

I MUST NOT ATTEMPT TO CONTROL GOD'S actions; I must not count the stages in the journey he would have me make. I must not desire a clear perception of my advance along the road, nor know precisely where I am on the way of holiness. I ask him to make a saint of me, yet I must leave to him the choice of that saintliness itself and still more the choice of the means that lead to it.

─────── DAY 117 ───────

IN OUR MEDITATIONS WE SHOULD ALWAYS ASK Jesus, "Make me a saint according to your own heart, meek and humble." "Learn of me," he insisted. We must say it in the spirit in which he meant it. We know him better now through our gospel lessons and meditations, but have we understood him in his humility? Does his humility appeal to us? Attract us?

OUR SOULS SHOULD BE LIKE A CLEAR GLASS through which God can be seen. Often this glass becomes spotted with dust and dirt. It is to remove this dirt and dust that our examen is made, so that I become once more "clean of heart" and able "to see God." He can, and he will help us to remove this "dirt and dust" if we sincerely will allow him to do it.

———————— DAY 119 ————————

WE COOK FOR NINE THOUSAND PEOPLE EVERY day. One day one sister came and said, "Mother, there's nothing to eat, nothing to give to the people." I had no answer. And then by nine o'clock that morning a truck full of bread came to our house. The government gives a slice of bread and milk to the poor children. That day—no one in the city knew why—suddenly all the schools were closed. And all the bread came to Mother Teresa. See, God closed the schools. He would not let our people go without food. And this was the first time, I think, in their lives that they had had such good bread and so much. This way you can see the tenderness of God.

---DAY 120---

HOW WILL I BECOME HUMBLE? BY ACCEPTING every humiliation that comes to me, by accepting myself as I am, and by rejoicing at our infirmity. Naturally we don't like this, but confidence in God can do all things. It is our emptiness and lowliness that God needs and not our plenitude. A fervent sister is conscious of her own weakness and tries to be happy when others see her weakness.

---DAY 121---

IN EACH OF OUR LIVES JESUS COMES AS THE Bread of Life to be eaten, to be consumed by us. This is how he loves us. Then Jesus comes in our human life as the hungry one, the other, hoping to be fed with the bread of our life, of our hearts by loving, and of our hands by serving. And in so doing we prove that we have been created in the likeness of God, for God is love and when we love we are like God. This is what Jesus meant when he said, "Be perfect as your Father in heaven is perfect" (Matthew 5:48, paraphrased).

DAY 122

IT IS VERY, VERY IMPORTANT FOR US TO HAVE A deep love for our Lady. For she was the one who taught Jesus how to walk, how to pray, how to wash, how to do all the little things that make our human life so beautiful. She had to do them. And the same thing now. She will always be willing to help us and teach us how to be all for Jesus alone, how to love only Jesus, how to touch him and see him, to serve him in the distressing disguise.

DAY 123

MARY WAS A TRUE MISSIONARY OF CHARITY because she was not afraid to be the handmaid of the Lord. She went in haste to put her beautiful humility into a living action of love, to do the handmaid's work for Elizabeth. We know what this humility obtained for the unborn child: he "leapt with joy" in the womb of his mother—the first human being to recognize the coming of Christ; and then his mother sang with joy, with gratitude, and praise.

DAY 124

OUR CLOTHING SHOULD BE RESPECTABLE IN order not to displease secular persons and repel them from our service. Yet our clothing must not be handsome or made from fine material. For reasons of health or due to climate we may have to increase the number of garments, but we should have nothing superfluous. However, we must beware not to mistake want of cleanliness, tidiness, or neatness for poverty. Dirty, uncared-for clothes are a sign of laziness and riches. They help neither health nor edification. Saint Bernard used to say: "I love poverty, not dirt."

DAY 125

NO ONE HAS LEARNED SO WELL THE LESSON OF humility as Mary did. She, being the handmaid of the Lord, was completely empty of self, and God filled her with grace. "Full of grace" means full of God. A handmaid is at someone's disposal, to be used according to some-one's wish with full trust and joy, to belong to someone without reserve. This is one main reason for the spirit of the Society.

Total surrender: to be at God's disposal, to be used as it pleases him, to be his handmaid, to belong to him.

—————DAY 126—————

SHE WILL TEACH US HER HUMILITY: THOUGH full of grace yet only the handmaid of the Lord; though the mother of God yet serving like a handmaid in the house of Elizabeth; though immaculately conceived, she meets Jesus humiliated, carrying his cross, and near the cross she stands as one of us, as if she were a sinner needing redemption.

Like her, the greater are the graces we have received, let us with greater and more delicate love touch the lepers, the dying, the lonely, the unwanted.

Like her, let us always accept the cross in whatever way it may come. Humility of the heart of Mary, fill my heart. Teach me as you taught Jesus to be meek and humble of heart and so glorify our Father.

—DAY 127—

AT HOLY COMMUNION WE DON'T SING ANY KIND of song. There should be perfect silence so that you can be alone with Jesus; it is the most precious time of the day. "Jesus, I believe in your tender love for me, I love you." It is really true at that time. He is really in your heart. Jesus came into Mary as he comes into us in Holy Communion. This is your chance to talk to him. Don't be in a hurry to get back to your place to start singing—maybe you have something special to say to him, "Yesterday, I was like that," or a special joy to share with him. Use his name. . . . After Communion try to be really alone with him. Talk to him, so that he can really possess you.

—DAY 128—

HOW MUCH WE CAN LEARN FROM OUR LADY! SHE was so humble because she was all for God. She was full of grace. She made use of the almighty power that was in her: the grace of God.

WHO IS JESUS TO ME?

Jesus is the Word made flesh.

Jesus is the Bread of Life.

Jesus is the victim offered for our sins on the cross.

Jesus is the sacrifice offered at holy Mass for the sins of the world and for mine.

Jesus is the word to be spoken.

Jesus is the truth to be told.

Jesus is the way to be walked.

Jesus is the light to be lit.

Jesus is the life to be lived.

Jesus is the love to be loved.

Jesus is the joy to be shared.

Jesus is the sacrifice to be offered.

Jesus is the peace to be given.

Jesus is the Bread of Life to be eaten.

Jesus is the hungry to be fed.

Jesus is the thirsty to be satiated.

Jesus is the naked to be clothed.

Jesus is the homeless to be taken in.

Jesus is the sick to be healed.

Jesus is the lonely to be loved.

Jesus is the unwanted to be wanted.

Jesus is the leper to wash his wounds.

Jesus is the beggar to give him a smile.

Jesus is the drunkard to listen to him.

Jesus is the mentally ill to protect him.

Jesus is the little one to embrace him.

Jesus is the blind to lead him.

Jesus is the dumb to speak for him.

Jesus is the crippled to walk with him.

Jesus is the drug addict to befriend him.

Jesus is the prostitute to remove from danger and befriend her.

Jesus is the prisoner to be visited.

Jesus is the old to be served.

DAY 130

FIDELITY IN THE LEAST THINGS, NOT FOR THEIR own sake—for this is the work of small minds—but for the sake of the great thing, which is the will of God and which I respect greatly in little things. Saint Augustine said: "Little things are indeed little, but to be faithful in little things is a great thing." Is not our Lord equally the same in a small host as in a great one? The smallest rule contains the will of God as much as the big things of life.

——————DAY 131——————

IN THEIR VISITS LET THE SISTERS ENCOURAGE true devotion to the Sacred Heart and the family rosary. They should induce the Catholic families to be consecrated to the Sacred Heart and to the Immaculate Heart of Mary. We have to try our utmost to keep the families together, remembering that "the family that prays together stays together." There are so many broken homes—the wife here, the husband there. Teach them that happiness can't be found without prayer. Even in old age there is no security against temptation.

——————DAY 132——————

DURING THIS TIME OF GRACE LET US, IN A SPE- cial way, ask our Lady to teach us her silence, her kindness, her humility.

Silence of Mary, speak to me, teach me how with you

and like you I can learn to keep all things in my heart as you did, not to answer back when accused or corrected as you did, to pray always in the silence of my heart as you did.

DAY 133

"TO LABOR AT THE CONVERSION AND SANCTIFICAtion of the poor in the slums." To labor, meaning hard, ceaseless toiling, without results, without counting cost. "To convert" is to bring to God. "To sanctify" means to feel with God. To convert and sanctify is the work of God, but God has chosen in his great mercy the Missionaries of Charity to help him in his own work.

DAY 134

LET US NOT FORGET THAT HUMILITY WE OWE God out of reverence to him. Secondly that our humility is not only an imitation of Christ but also a perfect way of giving oneself to Jesus, for when we are able to accept with joy all these humiliations, love for Jesus becomes very intimate and very ardent.

—DAY 135—

LET THE SISTERS BRING THE CHILDREN TO MASS.
Do your best to get them. If you have to run for a child,
do it, and God in his infinite mercy may give the light
and grace to that soul because of all the trouble you took.
Never lose sight of the mercy of God. Take the trouble to
help the children to love the Mass, to know the meaning of
the Mass, to join in the Mass through simple prayers and
hymns. Be careful of the attitude you take while mind-
ing the children during Mass. Do not correct loudly. Keep
your hands joined. Join in the prayers and the singing. The
children will do exactly what you do.

—DAY 136—

JOY IS PRAYER; JOY IS STRENGTH; JOY IS LOVE, A
net of love by which you can catch many souls. God loves
a cheerful giver. He gives most who gives with joy. If in the
work you have difficulties and you accept them with joy,
with a big smile, in this, as in any other good thing, "they
will see your good works and glorify the Father" (Matthew

5:16, paraphrased). The best way to show your gratitude to God and people is to accept everything with joy. A joyful heart is the normal result of a heart burning with love.

—————DAY 137—————

SILENCE GIVES US A NEW OUTLOOK ON EVERY-thing. We need silence to be able to touch souls. The essential thing is not what we say but what God says to us and through us. Jesus is always waiting for us in silence. In that silence, he will listen to us, there he will speak to our soul, and there we will hear his voice.

—————DAY 138—————

JESUS WANTS US TO BE HOLY AS HIS FATHER IS. We can become very great saints if we only want to. Holiness is not the luxury of the few, but a simple duty for you and for me.

DAY 139

WHILE WE ARE PREPARING FOR THE COMING OF the Holy Spirit, I pray for you that the Holy Spirit may fill you with his purity, so that you can see the face of God in each other and in the faces of the poor you serve. I ask the Holy Spirit to free you of all impurity—body, soul, mind, will, and heart—that each of you become the living tabernacle of God Most High, and so become a carrier of God's love and compassion. Ask the Holy Spirit to make you a sinner without sin.

DAY 140

SILENCE OF THE TONGUE WILL TEACH US SO MUCH: to speak to Christ, to be joyful at recreation, and to have many things to say. At recreation Christ speaks to us through others, and at meditation he speaks to us directly. Silence also makes us so much more Christlike because he had a special love for this virtue.

---DAY 141---

OUR LIVES, TO BE FRUITFUL, MUST BE FULL OF Christ; to be able to bring his peace, joy, and love, we must have it ourselves, for we cannot give what we have not got—the blind leading the blind. The poor in the slums are without Jesus and we have the privilege of entering their homes. What they think of us does not matter, but what we are to them does matter. To go to the slums merely for the sake of going will not be enough to draw them to Jesus. If you are preoccupied with yourself and your own affairs, you will not be able to live up to this ideal.

---DAY 142---

IF YOU GIVE TO THE PEOPLE A BROKEN CHRIST, A lame Christ, a crooked Christ, deformed by you, that is all they will have. If you want them to love him, they must know him first. Therefore, give the whole Christ first to the sisters, then to the people in the slums: Christ, full of zeal, love, joy, and sunshine. Do I come up to the mark? Am I a dark light, a false light, a bulb without the connection, having no current, therefore shedding no radiance? Put your heart into being a bright light. Say to Christ, "Help me to shed thy fragrance everywhere I go." Our very name explains this rule: sisters of the slums, carriers of Christ's love.

—DAY 143—

IN THE SLUMS THE SISTERS SHOULD FIND A place where they will gather the little street children, whoever they may be. Their first concern is to make them clean, feed them, and only then teach them, just a little reading and writing. Religion must be proposed to them in a simple, interesting, and attractive way. Whatever the sisters teach, first there must always be something the children can enjoy and yet at the same time learn.

—DAY 144—

WE NEED A VERY DEEP LIFE OF PRAYER TO BE able to love as he loves each one of us. We must ask our Lady, "Dear mother, teach me to love, prepare me." It's not enough just to join a priesthood. . . . That's not enough. We need to be more and more humble like Mary and holy like Jesus. [Only if] we are humble like Mary, we can be holy like Jesus. That's all: holy like the Lord.

—DAY 145—

WE READ IN THE GOSPEL THAT GOD LOVED THE world so much that he gave his Son Jesus through Mary the Most Pure. Our Lady didn't understand, but "Be it done to me" was her reply, a humble obedience (Luke 1:38 DRA). Nobody could have been a better priest than our Lady, and yet she remained only the handmaid of the Lord.

—DAY 146—

AND IF TODAY WE HAVE SO MUCH DIFFICULTY IN the world, it is because in our family we are not praying together. We have so many broken homes, so many separated families, why? Because the love has died, because we are not praying. So let us bring prayer back again in our family. Ask your teachers to teach your children. Ask, I ask you parents, teach your children how to pray and pray with them.

DAY 147

WHEN VISITING THE FAMILIES, YOU WILL MEET with very much misery. Sometimes you will find a little child watching near a dying parent, or holding the head of a dead parent. It is then that you must put out all your energy to help that little child in his sorrow. Once there were found two little children near the dead body of their father, who had died two days before. Thank God, sisters came and rescued the children and arranged a proper burial for the father.

DAY 148

NIRMAL HRIDAY IS BENGALI FOR "PURE HEART," and is the first home for the dying that Mother Teresa named after Mary's Immaculate Heart. Nirmal Hriday is only a means. If it were only a matter of washing and cleaning, it would be closed today. But for the opportunities it affords to reach souls, it is most important. In Nirmal Hriday we understand better the value of a soul.

—————————DAY 149—————————

SOMETIME BACK, I PICKED UP THIS MAN OFF THE street, covered with dirt and worms. He was eaten up alive. The only part of his body that was clean was his face. There were crawling worms on his body. I took him to our home. And he said then, "I have lived like an animal in the street. I am going to die like an angel, loved and cared for." It took us three hours to clean him, to remove everything from his body. And then he said, "Sister, I am going home to God." And he died. He really went home to God with such a beautiful smile on his face. I've never seen a smile like that. There was this man who had lived like an animal in the streets, eaten up alive by worms. And yet, he had courage. And he was looking forward. There was peace and joy in his face because somebody loved him, somebody wanted him, somebody helped him to die in peace with God.

—DAY 150—

RECENTLY, ONE GREAT BRAZILIAN MAN, A MAN OF high position, wrote to me that he had lost total faith in God and in man. He gave up his position and everything, even watching television, and he only wanted to commit suicide. One day, as he was passing by a shop, his eyes suddenly fell on the television. There was the scene of Nirmal Hriday, the sisters looking after the sick and dying. He wrote to me that after seeing that scene, for the first time after many years, he knelt and prayed. Now he has decided to turn back to God and have faith in humanity because he saw God still loves the world—he saw this on the television.

—DAY 151—

THE VERY FACT THAT GOD HAS PLACED A CERtain soul in your way is a sign that God wants to do something for her. It is not chance. It has been planned by God. We are bound in conscience to help. If a soul desires God, she has the right to be given the means to go to him.

No one has the right to stand between. Look at the cross and you will know what one soul means to Jesus.

—DAY 152—

ZEAL FOR SOULS IS THE EFFECT AND THE PROOF of true love of God. We cannot but be consumed with the desire for saving souls, the greatest and dearest interest of Jesus. Therefore, zeal is the test of love, and the test of zeal is devotedness to his cause, spending life and energy in the work of souls.

—DAY 153—

"THOU SHALT LOVE THE LORD THY GOD WITH all thy heart, and with all thy soul, and with all thy mind" (Matthew 22:37 KJV). This is the command of the great God, and he cannot command the impossible. Love is a fruit, in season at all times and within the reach of every hand. Anyone may gather it and no limit is set. Everyone can reach this love through meditation, the spirit of prayer, and sacrifices, by an intense interior life. Do I really live this life?

─────────────DAY 154─────────────

OBEDIENCE WELL LIVED FREES US FROM SELF-ishness and pride and so it helps us to find God and in him the whole world. Obedience is a special grace and it produces unfailing peace, inward joy, and close union with God.

─────────────DAY 155─────────────

TO POSSESS GOD WE MUST ALLOW HIM TO POS-sess our soul. How poor we would be if God had not given us the power of giving ourselves to him; how rich we are now! And how easy it is to conquer God! We give ourselves to God, then God is ours, and there can be nothing more ours than God. The money with which God repays our surrender is himself. We become worthy of possessing him when we abandon ourselves completely to him.

DAY 156

JESUS HAS CHOSEN US FOR HIMSELF; WE BELONG to him. Let us be so convinced of this belonging that we do not allow, nor accept anything, however small, to separate us from this belonging, from this love.

DAY 157

TO SURRENDER MEANS TO OFFER HIM MY FREE will, and my reason, or that is my own light, to be guided by God's word in pure faith. My soul may be in darkness, but I know that darkness, trial, and suffering are the surest test of my blind surrender.

DAY 158

SURRENDER IS ALSO TRUE LOVE. THE MORE WE surrender, the more we love God and souls. If we really love souls, we must be ready to take their place, to take their sins upon us and expiate them in us by penance and continual mortification. We must be living holocausts, for the souls need us as such.

<hr>

DAY 159

THERE IS NO LIMIT TO GOD'S LOVE. IT IS WITHout measure and its depth cannot be sounded. This is shown by his living and dying among us. Now turn the same picture around. There must be no limit to the love that prompts us to give ourselves to God, to be the victim of his unwanted love, that is, the love of God that has not been accepted by men.

<hr>

DAY 160

THE MISSIONARY OF CHARITY, IN ORDER TO BE true to her name, must be full of charity in her own soul and spread that same charity to the souls of others, Christians and pagans.

DAY 161

SOMEONE ONCE ASKED ME, "ARE YOU MARRIED?" And I said, "Yes, and I find it sometimes very difficult to smile at Jesus because he can be very demanding sometimes." This is really something true. And there is where love comes, when it is demanding, and yet we can give it to him with joy.

DAY 162

TOTAL SURRENDER CONSISTS IN GIVING OURselves completely to God. Why must we give ourselves fully to God? Because God has given himself to us. If God who owes nothing to us is ready to impart to us no less than himself, shall we answer with just a fraction of ourselves? To give ourselves fully to God is a means of receiving God himself. I for God and God for me. I live for God and give up my own self, and in this way induce God to live for me.

DAY 163

OUR HOLY FAITH IS NOTHING BUT A GOSPEL OF love, revealing to us God's love for all and claiming in return humanity's love for God. "God is love": a missionary must be a missionary of love (1 John 4:8 KJV). We must spread God's love on earth if we want to make souls repent whole-heartedly for sin, to strengthen them in temptation, and to increase their generosity and their desire to suffer for Christ. Let us act as Christ's love among men, remembering the words of *The Imitation*, "Love feels no burden, values no labors, would willingly do more than it can, complains not of impossibilities, because it conceives that it may and can do all things; when weary is not tired; when strained is not constrained; when frightened is not disturbed; but like a living flame and torch all on fire, it mounts upwards and securely passes through all opposition."

DAY 164

IN OUR WORK WE MAY OFTEN BE CAUGHT IN THE dangerous nets of the devil, idle conversations or . . . gossip. Let us be well on our guard, for we may be caught while visiting families. We may talk about the private affairs of this or that one and so forget the real aim of our visit. We come to bring the peace of Christ, and what if we are a cause of trouble? How our Lord will be hurt by such conduct! We must never allow people to speak against priests, religious, or their neighbors.

DAY 165

IF WE FIND THAT A FAMILY IS IN A BAD MOOD AND is sure to start a tale of uncharitableness, let us say a fervent prayer for them and then say a few things that may help them to think a little about God; then let us leave the place at once. We can do no good until their restless nerves are at peace. We must follow the same conduct with those who want to talk with the aim of wasting our precious time.

DAY 166

LOVE BEGINS AT HOME. EVERYTHING DEPENDS on how we love each other. Make your community live on this love and spread the fragrance of Jesus' love everywhere you go. Do not be afraid to love until it hurts, for this is how Jesus loved.

DAY 167

BE KIND AND LOVING WITH EACH OTHER, FOR you cannot love Christ in his distressing disguise if you cannot love Jesus in the heart of your brothers and sisters. Love, to be living, must be fed on sacrifice. Be generous with the penances and all the sacrifices that come from our poverty, and you will be able in all sincerity to say, "My God and my all."

DAY 168

THE MORE I GO AROUND, THE BETTER I UNDER-stand how very necessary it is for us to pray the work, to make the work our love for God in action. To be able to do that, how necessary it is to live that life of total surrender to God, loving trust in our superior and in each other, and cheerfulness with the poor.

DAY 169

IT IS NOT POSSIBLE TO ENGAGE IN THE DIRECT apostolate without being a soul of prayer, without a conscious awareness and submission to the divine will.

DAY 170

WE MUST BECOME HOLY NOT BECAUSE WE WANT to feel holy but because Christ must be able to live his life fully in us. We are to be all love, all faith, all purity for the sake of the poor we serve. Once we have learned to seek first God and his will, our contacts with the poor will become the means of great sanctity to ourselves and to others. Holiness is union with God; so in prayer and action alike, we come from God in Christ and go to God through Christ.

DAY 171

ONE DAY SAINT MARGARET MARY ASKED JESUS, "Lord, what wilt thou have me to do?" "Give me a free hand," Jesus answered. He will perform the divine work of sanctity, not you, and he asks only for your docility. Let him empty and amend you, and afterward fill the chalice of your heart to the brim, that you in your turn may give of your abundance. See him in the tabernacle; fix your eyes on him who is the light; bring your hearts close to his divine heart; ask him to grant you the grace of knowing him, the love of loving him, the courage to serve him. Seek him fervently.

DAY 172

LET US ALL MAKE REPARATION BY OUR FIDELITY to penance, life of sacrifices and life of prayer, fidelity to the work [for] the poor. Our fidelity is our reparation, and we will be able to make up for all our sins and the sins of the world. Again and again, in all the masses, [in] all the chapels and churches, are offered two or three consecrations every second. You can offer the Precious Blood with some sacrifices—little sacrifices.

DAY 173

WE MUST ALSO BE ABLE TO MAKE THE DISTINCtion between self-knowledge and sin. Self-knowledge will help us to rise up, whereas sin and the weakness that leads to repeated sin will lead to despondency. Deep confidence and trust will come through self-knowledge. Then you will turn to Jesus to support you in your weakness, whereas if you think you are strong, you will not need our Lord.

DAY 174

KNOWLEDGE OF CHRIST, AND HIM IN HIS POOR, will lead us to personal love. This love only can become our light and joy in cheerful service of each other. Do not forget we need each other. Our lives would be empty without each other. How can we love God and his poor if we do not love each other with whom we live and break the bread of life daily?

DAY 175

JUST TO MAKE LOVE MORE REAL, HE GIVES HIM-self in the Eucharist. What more could he do than this? Jesus is there. Say that prayer: "Jesus in my heart, I believe in your tender love for me, I love you." He is there and if you know that he is there, all your life will change. Say again and again: "Jesus in my heart, I believe in your tender love for me, I love you." Show that love in action, take care of each other.

DAY 176

WE MUST KNOW EXACTLY WHEN WE SAY YES TO God what that yes means. Yes means "I surrender," totally, fully, without any counting the cost, without any examination. Is it all right or convenient? Yes to God, without any reservations, and being contemplative that I belong to him so totally that there are no reservations; it doesn't matter what we feel, but that he feels all right. That yes is total surrender.

DAY 177

WHEN COMMUNICATING WITH CHRIST IN YOUR heart after partaking of the Living Bread, remember what our Lady must have felt when the Holy Spirit overpowered her, and she who was full of grace became full with the body of Christ. The spirit in her was so strong that immediately she "rose in haste" to go and serve.

DAY 178

IN THE SCRIPTURE WE READ OF THE TENDERness of God for the world, and we read that God loved the world so much that he gave his Son Jesus to come to be like us and to bring us the good news that God is love, that God loves you and loves me. God wants us to love each other as he loves each one of us. We all know, when we look at the cross, how Jesus loved us. When we look at the Eucharist, we know how he loves us now. That's why he made himself the Bread of Life, to satisfy our hunger for his love, and then, as if this was not enough for him, he made himself the hungry one, the naked one, the homeless one, so that you and I can satisfy his hunger for our human love. For we have been created for that. We have been created to love and to be loved.

—DAY 179—

WHERE WILL YOU GET THE JOY OF LOVING? IN the Eucharist, Holy Communion. Jesus has made himself the Bread of Life to give us life. Night and day, he is there. If you really want to grow in love, come back to the Eucharist, come back to that adoration. I have seen in our congregation, we used to have adoration once a week for one hour, and then in 1973, we decided to have adoration one hour every day. We have much work to do. Our homes for the sick and dying and destitute are full everywhere, and yet, around the time we started having adoration every day, our love for Jesus is more intimate, our love for each other more understanding, our love for the poor more compassionate, and we have double the number of vocations. God has blessed us with many wonderful vocations.

SAINT THÉRÈSE, THE LITTLE FLOWER, EXPLAINED surrender very beautifully. She said, "I am like a little ball in the hand of Jesus. He plays with me. He throws me away, puts me in the corner. And then like a little child who wants to see what is inside, he tears the ball apart and throws the pieces away." This is what a brother of the Word has to be, that little ball in the hand of Jesus. This expresses really that total surrender, which is the spirit of the carriers of God's love. We carry God's love in action, you carry God's love in word but [we are] carriers—missionaries. But it is one mission, the mission of love and compassion.

DAY 181

EACH MORNING I, TOO, MUST BE IN HASTE: I AM going to have an audience with God. Each morning I receive Jesus: his blood, his body in my body. What happens? Our Lady spent nine months with Jesus; in her was Jesus . . . and what did she do? Rub, scrub, clean, wash, but she really loved her total surrender. I have to do the same. In the street, go in haste, burning with love—zeal—to give Jesus.

—DAY 182—

TO BECOME HOLY WE NEED HUMILITY AND prayer. Jesus taught us how to pray, and he also told us to learn from him to be meek and humble of heart. Neither of these can we do unless we know what is silence. Both humility and prayer grow from a heart, mind, and tongue that have lived in silence with God, for in the silence of the heart God speaks.

—DAY 183—

OUR VOCATION IS TO BELONG TO JESUS, TO BELONG with a conviction, not because my vocation is to work with the poor or to be a contemplative, but because I am called to belong to him in the conviction that nothing can separate me from his love. This is what will make you contemplative brothers, that belonging with that conviction, and the fruit of that belonging will be your vow of chastity, the freedom of your poverty, the total surrender in obedience, and, especially . . . that wholehearted free service of the Word for the spiritually poorest of the poor.

<hr>—DAY 184—<hr>

ALL THE RELIGIOUS CONGREGATIONS—NUNS, priests, even the Holy Father—all have the same vocation: to belong to Jesus. "I have chosen you to be mine." That's our vocation. Our means: that I spend time in the service to the poor, that you spend time in adoration, that is [a] means. Our love for Jesus in action is only the means, just like clothes. I wear this, you wear that: it's a means. But vocation is not a means; vocation is Jesus.

<hr>—DAY 185—<hr>

OUR ACTIVE BROTHERS AND SISTERS PUT THAT love into action in service, and contemplative brothers and sisters put that love into action in prayer, in penance, in adoration, in contemplation, and in proclaiming the Word that they have meditated, that you have contemplated, that you have adored—that Word you have to give. Active and contemplative are not two different lives; it is only that one is faith in action through service, the other faith in action through prayer.

—DAY 186—

FAITH IN ACTION THROUGH PRAYER, FAITH IN action through service, but it is the same faith, the same love, same compassion. We have to proclaim that faith, we have to proclaim that one Christ, only we are using different means. This is something that should encourage us and should be a strength for us, that we complete each other more fully. . . . Because we are human beings, we need these names and these separations, and things like that. But the soul, the mind, and the heart has that one thing: total surrender to God. At the moment we realize that we have really done that, then we are at his disposal, and there are no more differences.

—————————DAY 187—————————

AND THIS EXPRESSES REALLY THAT TOTAL SUR-
render, which is the spirit of the carriers of God's love.
We the sisters carry God's love in action, you brothers of
the Word carry God's love in word, but we are both carriers, we both are missionaries. The mission of proclaiming
Christ, through action or through words, is one mission,
the mission of love and compassion. For the sake of making things simpler you have different names, but this is just
for external reasons. Actually, it is the same thing: we both
work for the proclamation of God's kingdom.

—————————DAY 188—————————

RIGHT FROM THE BEGINNING, BROTHERS, TAKE
the trouble to listen to the voice of God in prayer, in adoration, and in contemplation. You may go out into the street
and have nothing to say. All right, but maybe there is a
man sitting there on the corner and you go to him. Maybe
he resents you, but you are there, and that presence is there.
You must radiate that presence that is within you, in the

way you address that man with love and respect. Why? Because you believe that is Jesus. Jesus cannot deceive you: of this you must be convinced. He comes disguised in the form of that person there. This is our fourth vow. You are bound by the same vow, only with us sisters, this hunger is more on the material side, and for you brothers it is spiritual hunger, spiritual nakedness, spiritual homelessness. Believe me, brothers, I find it much more difficult to work with people who have bitterness, who have anxiety in their hearts, who are unwanted, unloved, uncared for.

―――――――DAY 189―――――――

THE ESSENTIAL MUST BE THE SAME, THE SAME spirit of total surrender, the same satiating of the thirst of Jesus, the same proclamation, the same presence, the same poverty, the same chastity. The four vows must not be different. What you are doing, that love for Christ, that presence and that Word of God, we are putting into action. It is the same thing. You are to be his presence with the Word, and we are sent to be his presence by action.

—DAY 190—

THIS IS WHAT WE HAVE TO LEARN RIGHT FROM the beginning, to listen to the voice of God in our heart, and then in the silence of the heart God speaks. Then from the fullness of our hearts, our mouth will have to speak. That is the connection. . . . In the silence of the heart, God speaks and you have to listen. Then in the fullness of your heart, because it is full of God, full of love, full of compassion, full of faith, your mouth will speak. . . .

Listen in silence, because if your heart is full of other things, you cannot hear the voice of God. But when you have listened to the voice of God in the silence of your heart, then your heart is filled with God, like our Lady full of grace. And then "from the fullness of the heart the mouth speaks" (Luke 6:45 NAB).

—DAY 191—

YOU MAY BE WRITING, AND THE FULLNESS OF your heart will come to your hand also. Your heart may speak through writing. Your heart may speak through your eyes also. You know that when you look at people they must be able to see God in your eyes. If you go down like this (get distracted and worldly), then they will not be able to see God like that. The fullness of our heart is expressed in our eyes, in our touch, in what we write, in what we say, in the way we walk, in the way we receive, in the way we need. That is the fullness of our heart expressing itself in many different ways.

————————DAY 192————————

IT'S NOT ENOUGH JUST TO GO AND BECOME A brother. That's not enough. But it's very important for us to allow Jesus to live his life of love, of prayer, of oneness with the Father. God speaks in the silence of the heart, and we listen. And then we speak to God from the fullness of our heart, and God listens. And this listening and this speaking is what prayer is meant to be: that oneness with God, that oneness with Jesus.

—DAY 193—

AS A CONTEMPLATIVE, YOUR MOUTH MUST BE very pure to be able to utter those words of God all the time, just as our hands in our active life must be very pure when we touch the body of Christ. This is something that must be the very life of our life. Otherwise we could rattle off many things, and learn many things by heart, and know all possible knowledge, and all of theology and all the things about God, but we would not be able to light that fire in the hearts of the people. We are just uttering words, not living those words. That is why it is necessary for us that our words be the fruit of our life, the fruit of our prayers, the fruit of our penance, and the fruit of our adoration.

—DAY 194—

THERE IS A VERY IMPORTANT THEOLOGIAN, A very holy priest, who is also one of the best in India right now. I know him very well, and I said to him, "Father, you talk all day about God. How close you must be to God!

You are talking all the time about God." And you know what he said to me? He said, "I may be talking much about God, but I may be talking very little to God." And then he explained, "I may be rattling so many words and maybe saying many good things, but deep down I have not got the time to listen. Because in the silence of the heart, God speaks."

———————————DAY 195———————————

IT IS VERY IMPORTANT THAT RIGHT FROM THE beginning, brothers, we simply live the gospel. Live the gospel in prayer; live the gospel in words. Don't be discouraged if you don't reach the height right away. There is no reason for us to be either upset or discouraged, but just one thing is important. That one thing may be nothing in comparison to what people outside expect from you, and yet if you do not put that little drop of prayer, of penance, in your life and in your heart, then the people will be without that. You won't be able to give what you don't have.

---DAY 196---

THE FULLNESS OF OUR HEART COMES IN OUR actions: how I treat that leper, how I treat that dying person, how I treat the homeless. Sometimes it is more difficult to work with the street people than with the people in our homes for the dying because the dying are peaceful and waiting; they are ready to go to God. You can touch the sick and believe, or you can touch the leper and believe that it is the body of Christ you are touching, but it is much more difficult when these people are drunk or shouting to think that this is Jesus in that distressing disguise. How clean and loving our hands must be to be able to bring that compassion to them!

---DAY 197---

YOU IN THE WEST HAVE THE SPIRITUALLY POOR-est of the poor much more than you have physically poor people. Very often among the rich there are very, very spiritually poor people. I find no difficulty in giving a plate of rice to a hungry person, or a bed to a person who has no bed, but to console or to remove that bitterness, to remove that anger, to remove that loneliness takes a long time.

---DAY 198---

JESUS HAS MADE HIMSELF THE BREAD OF LIFE to satisfy my hunger for him, and he has also made himself the hungry one so that I may satisfy his love for me. He is hungry for us just as we are hungry for him. The Word has to become flesh among you—in love, in unity, in peace, in joy, and then you will be able to give it to the spiritually poorest, to give it to that man sitting in the park, drunk and all by himself.

---DAY 199---

JESUS HAS CHOSEN US IN A SPECIAL WAY TO enter Nazareth . . . just to live the Word of God, to believe in the Word; that Word has life, and that we give the Word of Life, Jesus, to all we meet, beginning with our own community, for love begins at home. How does it begin at home? By praying together; a family that prays together stays together.

AND IF YOU PRAY TOGETHER, YOU WILL STAY together. You will be that presence of Christ to each other. Love each other tenderly as Jesus loves each one of you. That is the holiness: tender love for each other that speaks much louder than all the words you can say. Love until it hurts; it takes deep sacrifice to proclaim the Word of God. Never hurt anybody with a word, which is so sacred in your mouth. The most important thing is that whatever you say you really live it: the younger brothers that come up learn by seeing, not so much by hearing. Now young people don't bother to listen, they want to see.

——————DAY 201——————

YOU BROTHERS WHO IN A SPECIAL WAY HAVE taken the Word of God, how clean your heart must be to be able to speak from the fullness of your heart! But before you speak, it is necessary for you to listen, for God speaks in the silence of the heart. You have to listen, and only then, from the fullness of your heart, you speak and God listens.

DAY 202

BY YOUR PRESENCE YOU MUST BE THE LIGHT. Christ must be the light, according to the prayer that we say, "Shine through me so that your light might shine through me and then the people when they look up they will see only Jesus." We'll have a competition today, and our competition is with Jesus; he is there the light and we have to meet him, and that competition is that we take his light and light it in every heart that we meet, not in big groups or with big numbers . . . but in the street, in the hospitals, in the jails: any place where darkness has surrounded that person, you are to be the light there.

DAY 203

THERE IS A GREAT HUMILITY IN GOD. HE CAN stoop down to people like us and become dependent on us for these things to live, to grow, to bear fruit. And he could easily have done it without us. Yet he stooped down and took each of us here to call us together to make this community. And if you had refused, he couldn't have done it. We could have said no. Each of us could have said no and it would have ended there. God would have waited patiently for somebody who would say yes. This is what makes me realize that when Jesus said, "Learn of me, because I am meek, and humble of heart" (Matthew 11:29 DRA), he really meant that we should learn that humility from God himself, who stooped down to do all these things.

—DAY 204—

AND WHAT IS PERFECT LOVE OF GOD? HOLINESS, you must be holy. Holiness is the greatest gift that God can give us because for that reason he created us. For that reason you have become brothers. You have not come here just to spend time, even to spend your time praying. You have come here to be his love, his compassion. You have been sent.

THE AIM FOR US TO EXIST IS TO BE ABLE TO SATI-
ate that thirst, to be contemplative, by bringing the love
of the Word of God to the people. How pure, how clean
your heart must be, because from the fullness of the heart
you have to speak.

WHAT IS CONTEMPLATION? BEING ONE WITH
Jesus. This is what I understand: to allow Jesus to live his
life in us, to live our life in his life. That's contemplation.
We must have a clean heart to be able to see no jealousy,
anger, uncharitableness, and especially no uncharitableness. To me, contemplation is not to be shut up in a dark
place, but to allow Jesus to live his Passion, his love, his
compassion, his humility in us, praying with us, being
with us, sanctifying through us.

DAY 207

LOVE BEGINS AT HOME, LOVE BEGINS IN OUR community. We cannot love outside unless we really love our brothers and sisters inside. So I say we need a very clean heart to be able to see God. When we all see God in each other, we will love one another as he loves us all. That is the fulfillment of the law, to love one another. This is all Jesus came to teach us: that God loves us, and that he wants us to love one another as he loves us.

DAY 208

BROTHERS, TO GIVE THE WORD OF GOD, TO BE the Word of God to your people is the reason for your existence. But you cannot give, you cannot utter that Word unless you live that Word, unless you pray that Word. To be able to give, you must have. To that end you will stay holy, that you may understand what Jesus wants: to be through you and in you.

DAY 209

THE WORLD TODAY IS HUNGRY NOT ONLY FOR bread but hungry for love; hungry to be wanted, to be loved. They're hungry to feel that presence of Christ. In many countries, people have everything except that presence, that understanding love. That's why the life of prayer and sacrifice comes to give that love. By being contemplative, you are to be that presence, that bread of God to break.

DAY 210

PEOPLE ARE HUNGRY FOR THE WORD OF GOD that will give peace, that will give unity, that will give joy. But you cannot give what you don't have. That's why it is necessary to deepen your life of prayer. Allow Jesus to take you, pray with you and through you, and then you will be a real, true contemplative in the heart of the world.

DAY 211

WE ARE CALLED TO LOVE THE WORLD. AND GOD loved the world so much that he gave Jesus. Today he loves the world so much that he gives you and gives me to be his love, his compassion, and that presence, that life of prayer, of sacrifice, of surrender to God. And especially, brothers, this is what God wants from you: to be a contemplative. Actually, every single Christian, every Catholic who lives a life united in the Eucharist, united with Jesus, he is the contemplative, she is the contemplative.

DAY 212

WE HAVE A CONTEMPLATIVE HOUSE IN THE South Bronx. A taxi driver refused to take me there. The sisters did not know I was coming, so I had to take a taxi, but he refused to go there. I said, "But we are living there; our young sisters are living there." He said no. I said, "All right, I will sit near you and you will see that nothing will happen to either you or me." So I got in the taxi and we went. His mouth was open when he saw the young sisters jumping and laughing, and the people bowing, those who recognized me speaking to me; though they were drunk, they were taking off their hats, and so on. He couldn't get over it, seeing that presence. This is something very beautiful.

———DAY 213———

I REMEMBER THE FIRST TIME THE CONTEMPLA- tive sisters went into a New York park. They were dressed in white and they prayed the Rosary. When one man saw them, he said, "Oh, I'm not ready, I'm not ready." Then the sisters went a little closer to him and said, "We are sisters. Jesus loves you." He said, "I am not ready. You have come all the way from heaven, you are angels from heaven to take me. I am not ready." He thought that the angels had come to take him! That shows you what people expect of us.

DAY 214

OUR LADY WAS FULL OF GOD BECAUSE SHE LIVED for God alone, yet she thought of herself only as the handmaid of the Lord. Let us do the same.

DAY 215

THE CHURCH WANTS RENEWAL. RENEWAL DOES not mean changing of habit and a few prayers. Renewal is faithfulness to the spirit of the constitutions, a spirit that seeks holiness by means of a poor and humble life, the exercise of sincere and patient charity, spontaneous sacrifice and generosity of heart, and that finds its expression in purity and candor.

JESUS IS THE LIGHT
Jesus is the Truth
Jesus is the Life
We too must be:
the Light of Charity
the Truth of Humility
the Life of Sanctity

OUR WORKS OF LOVE ARE NOTHING BUT WORKS of peace. Let us do them with greater love and efficiency, each one in her own or his own work in daily life; in your home, in your neighborhood, it is always the same Christ who says, "I was hungry: not only for food but for peace that comes from a pure heart. I was thirsty: not for water but for peace that satiates the passionate thirst of passion for war. I was naked: not for clothes, but for that beautiful dignity of men and women for their bodies. I was homeless: not for a shelter made of bricks but for a heart that understands, that covers, that loves."

—DAY 218—

FOR LOVE TO BE TRUE, IT HAS TO HURT. GOD loved the world so much that he gave his Son. His Son loved the world so much that he gave his life. And Jesus says: "As the Father has loved me by giving me to the world, I have loved you by giving my life for you. Love as I have loved you, by giving yourself." This giving is prayer, the sacrifice of chastity, poverty, obedience, and whole-hearted free service.

—DAY 219—

PRAY LOVINGLY LIKE CHILDREN, WITH AN EAR-nest desire to love much and to make loved the Love that is not loved.

—DAY 220—

OUR PRAYERS ARE MOSTLY VOCAL PRAYERS; they should be burning words coming forth from the furnace of a heart filled with love. In these prayers, speak to God with great reverence and confidence. Pray with folded hands, downcast eyes, and lifted hearts, and your prayers will become like a pure sacrifice offered unto God. Do not drag or run ahead; do not shout or keep silent but devoutly, with great sweetness, with natural simplicity, without any affectation, offer your praise to God with the whole of your heart and soul. We must know the meaning of the prayers we say and feel the sweetness of each word to make these prayers of great profit; we must sometimes meditate on them and often during the day find our rest in them.

---DAY 221---

"WHATSOEVER YOU DID TO THE LEAST OF MY brethren, you did it to me" (Matthew 25:40, paraphrase). "This is my commandment, that you love one another" (John 15:12 RSV). Suppress this commandment and the whole grand work of the Church of Christ falls in ruins. For Jesus came to earth to give charity its rightful place in the hearts of men. "By this," he said, "men will know that you are my disciples, if you have love for one another" (John 13:35 RSV). And this commandment will last for all eternity. True love for our neighbor is to wish him well and to do good to him.

DAY 222

HEAR JESUS YOUR COWORKER SPEAK TO YOU: "I want you to be my fire of love among the poor, the sick, the dying, and the little children; the poor I want you to bring to me." Learn this sentence by heart and when you are wanting in generosity, repeat it. We can refuse Christ just as we refuse others: "I will not give you my hands to work with, my feet to walk with, my mind to study with, my heart to love with. You knock at the door, but I will not give you the key of my heart." This is what he feels so bitterly: not being able to live his life in a soul.

DAY 223

A FEW WEEKS AGO, I PICKED UP A CHILD FROM the street, and from the face I could see that little child was hungry. I don't know, I couldn't make out how many days that little one had not eaten. So I gave her a piece of bread, and the little one took the bread and, crumb by crumb, started eating it. I said to her, "Eat, eat the bread. You are hungry." And the little one looked at me and said, "I am afraid. When the bread is finished, I will be hungry again." The pain of hunger is something terrible. This little one has already experienced the pain of hunger, which maybe you have never experienced and will never experience. But remember, remember to share the joy of loving by giving until it hurts.

DAY 224

IF A BOY LEAVES HIS FATHER'S FIELD AND GOES to work on another, he is no longer his father's coworker. To be a coworker means to work along with someone, to share together in tiredness, humiliations, and shame, not only in success. Those who share everything are partners giving love for love, suffering for suffering. Jesus, you have died; you have given everything, life, blood, all. Now it is my turn. I put everything into the field also. The common soldier fights in the ordinary lines, but the devoted one tries to be near the captain to share his fate. This is the only truth, the only thing that matters, for it is the spirit of Christ.

I KNOW YOU ALL LOVE THE POOR—OTHERWISE you would not join—but let each one of us try to make this love more kind, more charitable, more cheerful. Let our eyes see more clearly in deep faith the face of Christ in the face of the poor.

OH, HOW BEAUTIFUL IT IS TO CONSOLE THE afflicted, to wait on the sick, to encourage and sustain, to cheer up the sad and the moody ones. The more we devote ourselves to these works of mercy, which are the means of satiating the thirst of Jesus for souls, the more will God love us. . . . In touching them how we have to think of Christ and touch him in them as the priest touches the appearances of bread that contains Christ's own body.

AS YOU KNOW, WE HAVE GOT OUR BROTHERS also who are Missionaries of Charity. One of our brothers loves the lepers. We are taking care of 49,000 lepers in India. This brother really loves the lepers. He came one day after he had had some difficulties with his superior. He said to me, "I love the lepers; I want to be with them. I want to work for them. My vocation is to be with the lepers." I said to him, "Brother, you are making a mistake. Your vocation is not to work for the lepers. Your vocation is to belong to Jesus. The work for the lepers is only your love for Christ in action; and therefore, it makes no difference to anyone as long as you are doing it to him, as long as you are doing it with him. That's all that matters. That is the completion of your vocation, of your belonging to Christ."

I WISH TO LIVE IN THIS WORLD, WHICH IS SO FAR from God, which has turned so much from the light of Jesus, to help them—our poor—to take upon me something of their sufferings. . . . Let us share the sufferings of our poor—for only by being one with them we can redeem them; that is, bringing God into their lives and bringing them to God.

DAY 229

WE MUST WORK IN GREAT FAITH, STEADILY, EFFIciently, and above all with great love and cheerfulness; for without this our work will be only the work of slaves serving a hard master.

DAY 230

WE SHOULD BE PROFESSIONALS IN PRAYER. THE apostles understood this very well. When they saw that they might be lost in a multitude of works, they decided to give themselves to continual prayer and to the ministry of the Word. We have to pray with those who pray and for those who do not pray.

JOHN'S DISCIPLES ALSO CAME TO ASK JESUS, "ARE you the Messiah or shall we wait for another?" The Bible tells us that Jesus answered them, saying, "Go and tell John: the blind see, the lame walk, the dumb speak, the lepers are cleansed, the dead rise, and the gospel is preached to the poor" (Luke 7:22, paraphrased). We are doing the same work. So wonderful is our vocation! By our works we also make Jesus present in our world of today. We proclaim that Jesus is the Christ, the Messiah, and he is in our midst. People kept on asking, "Who are you?" but Jesus did not answer them directly. He let the good work proclaim the good news and people meet God. They see God's love alive!

— DAY 232 —

WE ALL LONG FOR HEAVEN, WHERE GOD IS, BUT we have it in our power to be in heaven with him right now, to be happy with him at this very moment. But being happy with him now means loving like he loves, helping like he helps, giving as he gives, serving as he serves, rescuing as he rescues, and being with him twenty-four hours a day, touching him in his distressing disguise.

DAY 233

MY DEAR CHILDREN, WITHOUT OUR SUFFERING, our work would just be social work, very good and helpful, but it would not be the work of Jesus Christ, not part of the redemption. Jesus wanted to help us by sharing our life, our loneliness, our agony, and our death. All that he has taken upon himself, and has carried it in the darkest night; only by being one with us he has redeemed us. We are allowed to do the same; all the desolation of the poor people, not only their material poverty but also their spiritual destitution, must be redeemed, and we must have our share in it.

DAY 234

THE WORD OF GOD BECOMES FLESH DURING THE day, during your meditation, during Holy Communion, during contemplation, during adoration, during silence, during work. And that Word in you, you give to others. That is why it is necessary that the Word lives in you, that you understand the Word, that you love the Word, that you live the Word. You will not be able to give that Word unless you have it there.

—DAY 235—

LET EACH ONE OF US SEE JESUS CHRIST IN THE person of the poor. The more repugnant the work or the person the greater also must be our faith, love, and cheerful devotion ministering to our Lord in this distressing disguise.

—DAY 236—

TO LOVE MEANS TO GIVE, AND WE ARE EXPECTED to have total surrender; this spirit comes true in our relation with our poor people, for we are the missionaries, the carriers of God's own love. Charity for the poor must be a burning flame in our Society, and just as fire ceases to burn, it gives no more its usefulness and heat, so the

Society, the day it loses its grip on charity toward the poor, it will lose its usefulness; there will be no life.

DAY 237

JESUS SAYS, "WHATEVER YOU DO TO THE LEAST of your brothers is in my name. When you receive a little child you receive me. If in my name you give a glass of water, you give it to me." And to make sure that we understand what he is talking about, he says that at the hour of death we are going to be judged only that way. I was hungry, you gave me to eat. I was naked, you clothed me. I was homeless, you took me in. Hunger is not only for bread; hunger is for love. Nakedness is not only for a piece of clothing; nakedness is lack of human dignity, and also that beautiful virtue of purity, and lack of that respect for each other. Homelessness is not only being without a home made of bricks; homelessness is also being rejected, unwanted, unloved.

DAY 238

POPE PAUL SAYS THAT VOCATION MEANS THE capacity to heed the imploring voices of the world of innocent souls of those who suffer, who have no comfort, no guidance, no love. This requirement is beautifully fulfilled by our vow of wholehearted and free service to the poor. Just as Christ went about doing good, healing the sick, casting out devils, preaching the kingdom of God, we too spend ourselves untiringly in seeking, in towns as well as villages, even amid the dustbins, the poor, the abandoned, the sick, the infirm, the dying; and in taking care of them, helping them, visiting them, and giving them the message of Christ, and trying our best to bring them to God.

DAY 239

WE DO NOT ACCEPT POVERTY BECAUSE WE ARE forced to be poor but because we choose to be poor for the love of Jesus; because he, being rich, became poor for love of us (2 Corinthians 8:9). Let us not deceive ourselves. My sisters, do not bluff yourselves.

—DAY 240—

FAILURE AND LOSS OF VOCATION ALSO COME from neglect of prayer. And as prayer is the food of spiritual life, neglect of prayer starves the spiritual life and so loss of vocation is unavoidable. Let us ask our Lady in our own simple way to teach us how to pray, as she taught Jesus in all the years that he was with her in Nazareth.

—DAY 241—

WE MUST DO OUR UTMOST TO KEEP OUR SIGHT clear and free from the world so that our service to the poor may become one generous act of love. It is this "seeing" that made Father Damien the apostle of the lepers, that made Saint Vincent de Paul the father of the poor, that made each one of us give up all to serve the poor.

TO THE WORLD IT SEEMS FOOLISH THAT WE delight in poor food, that we relish rough and insipid bulgur; possess only three sets of habits made of coarse cloth or old soutanes, mend and patch them, take great care of them and refuse to have extra; enjoy walking in any shape and color of shoes; bathe with just a bucket of water in small bathing rooms; sweat and perspire but refuse to have a fan; go hungry and thirsty but refuse to eat in the houses of the people; refuse to have radios or phonographs, which could be relaxing to the racked nerves after the whole day's hard toil; walk distances in the rain and hot summer sun, or go cycling, travel by second-class tram, or third-class overcrowded trains; sleep on hard beds, giving up soft and thick mattresses, which would be soothing to the aching bodies after the whole day's hard work; kneel on the rough and thin carpets in the chapel, giving up soft and thick ones; delight in lying in the common wards in the hospital among the poor of Christ when we could easily have private cabins; work . . . at home and outside when we could easily employ servants and do only the light jobs; relish cleaning the toilets and dirt in the Nirmal Hriday [home for the dying] and Shishu Bhavan [home for the children]

as though that were the most beautiful job in the world, and call it all a tribute to God. To them we are wasting our precious life and burying our talents. Yes, our lives are utterly wasted if we use only the light of reason. Our life has no meaning unless we look at Christ in his poverty.

—————DAY 243—————

A MISSIONARY IS ONE SENT WITH A MISSION—A message to deliver. Just as Jesus was sent by his Father, we too are sent by him filled with his Spirit to be witnesses of his gospel of love and compassion in our communities first, and in our apostolate among the poorest of the poor all over the world.

—————DAY 244—————

OUR LORD GIVES US A LIVING EXAMPLE. "FOXES have holes, and the birds of the air have nests; but the Son of man hath not where to lay his head," Jesus said (Matthew 8:20 KJV). From the very first day of his human existence, he was brought up in poverty, which no other human being will ever be able to experience, because "being rich he made himself poor" (2 Corinthians 8:9, paraphrased). As I am his coworker *alter Christus*, I must be brought up and nourished by that poverty which our Lord asks of me.

DAY 245

TODAY, THERE IS SO MUCH SUFFERING, AND I feel that the Passion of Christ is being relived all over again. Are we there to share that passion, to share that suffering of people—around the world, not only in the poor countries. . . . So you must pray for us that we may be able to be that good news.

DAY 246

AM I CONVINCED THAT MY VOCATION IS A FOLlowing of Christ? Is it a conviction? That I "have been chosen"? I have not chosen—but he has chosen me.

KEEP THE LOVE FOR THE POOREST OF THE POOR always living. Do not think it is a waste of time to feed the hungry, to visit and take care of the sick and dying, to open homes and receive the unwanted and homeless. No, this is our love of Christ in action. The humbler the work, the greater must be your love and efficiency. Be not afraid of the life of sacrifice that comes from the life of poverty.

—DAY 248—

WE MAKE THE CHURCH PRESENT BY PROCLAIM-ing the good news. What is the good news? The good news is that God still loves the world through each one of you. You are God's good news; you are God's love in action. Through you God is still loving the world. So if you are a lazy missionary of charity, you will give a wrong picture of God's love in action. People are watching us constantly at all times, and they are meeting God's love in action by our touch of compassion and love to the poor in Nirmal Hriday, in Shishu Bhavan, to the leprosy patients, anywhere.

DAY 249

LET US RENEW OUR LOVE FOR OUR POOR. WE will be able to do so only if we are faithful to the poverty we have vowed, that we have chosen.

DAY 250

TO PRAY GENEROUSLY IS NOT ENOUGH; WE MUST pray devoutly, with fervor and piety. We must pray perseveringly and with great love.

DAY 251

THE GREATNESS OF OUR LADY WAS IN HER humility. No wonder Jesus, who lived so close to her, seemed to be so anxious that we learn from him and from her but one lesson: to be meek and humble of heart.

DAY 252

IT MAY HAPPEN THAT CHILDREN REPEATEDLY fail in their religious examination when being prepared for First Communion. Do not give in to discouragement. No more must you do so when you try to save a marriage or convert a sinner and you do not succeed. If you are discouraged, it is a sign of pride because it shows you trust in your own powers. Never bother about people's opinions. Be humble and you will never be disturbed.

DAY 253

WE DEPEND SOLELY ON DIVINE PROVIDENCE. WE don't accept government grants. We don't accept church maintenance, we don't accept salaries; nothing for the work. For we have consecrated our lives to give to the poorest of the poor wholehearted and free service and the joy of being loved. Our people are longing to be loved. And we have got that tenderness and love of God that is continually there.

DAY 254

IT IS IN LOVING OUR LORD AND OUR NEIGHBOR that our humility will flower, and it is in being humble that our love will become real, devoted, and ardent.

DAY 255

OUR LORD HAS A VERY SPECIAL LOVE FOR THE chaste. His own mother, Saint Joseph, and Saint John the beloved disciple all were consecrated to chastity. Why do I desire to be chaste? I want to be chaste because I am the spouse of Jesus Christ, the Son of the living God. I want to be chaste because of the work I have to do as the coworker of Christ. My chastity must be so pure as to draw the most impure to the Sacred Heart of Jesus.

DAY 256

WHEN AT HOME, THE SISTERS MUST KEEP THEM-selves very busy, working on the farm or making things for sale, for our Lord worked for his mother. He was a real laborer. He was known as the son of the carpenter; he lived a life of hard labor for nearly twenty years, never hesitating, never doubting the will of God, though he came to bring souls to God. In the hard work of his foster father's shop he showed the greatest virtues that a human being can have: humility, obedience, poverty. Always keeping himself above material preoccupations, he—the master of everything—worked not for the work itself but for him who sent him, for his Father in heaven.

DAY 257

THE SISTERS SHOULD NOT BE ASHAMED TO BEG from door to door if necessary, becoming beggars for the poor members of Christ, who himself lived on alms during his public life and whom they serve in the sick and poor.

DAY 258

"WHETHER YOU EAT OR SLEEP, DO IT ALL FOR the glory of God." Christ certainly did not feast sumptuously during his life. His parents were poor, and the poor do not feast on the good things of the table. In fact, he often endured real want, as the multiplication of the loaves and fishes and the plucking of the ears of grain on walks through the fields teach us. The thought of these instances should be salutary reminders when in the mission or at home our meals are meager. If dishes taste good, thank God; if not, thank him still and thank him even more because he has given you an opportunity to imitate our Savior in his poverty. It would be a defect to speak about food or to complain about what is served; to be occupied with such thoughts at any time is disedifying.

---DAY 259---

IN REALITY, THERE IS ONLY ONE TRUE PRAYER, only one substantial prayer: Christ himself. There is only one voice that rises above the face of the earth: the voice of Christ. The voice reunites and coordinates in itself all the voices . . . raised in prayer.

DAY 260

HOLINESS GROWS SO FAST WHERE THERE IS kindness. I have never heard of kind souls going astray. The world is lost for want of sweetness and kindness. In religious houses this kindness is in greater danger, for we have grown so much used to each other that some think they are free to say anything to anybody at any time. They expect the other sisters to bear with their unkindness. Why not try first to control your own tongue? You know what you can do, but you do not know how much the other can bear. Why not give the chance of holiness to yourself first? Your holiness will be of greater help to your sisters than the chance you give her to put up with your unkindness.

DAY 261

I THINK I'M NOT AFRAID FOR YOU BROTHERS IF you deepen your personal love for Christ. Then you will be all right. Then people may pass you by, but you will not be hurt, you will not be harmed. The first time you go out, they may throw stones at you, all right. Turn the other side. Let them throw at the other side also; what is important is that you are holding on, that you have got a grip on Christ and he will not let your hand go.

---DAY 262---

YES, MY DEAR CHILDREN, LET US ALL UNITE IN helping each other to become holy. For Jesus said, "Seek first the kingdom of God . . . and all these things will be added to you" (Matthew 6:33 ESV). The kingdom of God is holiness.

---DAY 263---

BE FAITHFUL IN LITTLE THINGS, FOR IN THEM our strength lies. To the good God nothing is little, because he is so great and we so small. That is why he stoops down and takes the trouble to make those little things for us, to give us a chance to prove our love for him. Because he makes them, they are very great. He cannot make anything small; they are infinite. Yes, my dear children, be faithful in little practices of love, of little sacrifices—of the little interior mortifications—of little fidelities to the rule, which will build in you the life of holiness and make you Christlike.

DAY 264

MY PRAYER FOR ALL FAMILIES IS THAT YOU grow in holiness through this love for each other. Bring Jesus wherever you go. Let them look up and see only Jesus in you. So pray for your children and pray that your daughters and sons will have the courage to say yes to God and to consecrate their lives totally to him. There are many, many families that would be so happy that their children would give their lives to God. So pray for them that they will be able to fulfill their hearts' desire.

DAY 265

BY THE VOW OF CHASTITY WE GIVE UP OUR hearts to our Lord, to the crucified Christ; the one place in our hearts belongs to him. In the Gospels, we read that God is like a jealous lover. We cannot have two masters, for we will serve one and hate the other. The vows themselves are but means of leading the soul to God, and the vow of chastity in particular is intended as a means of giving the heart to God. The heart is one of the highest and noblest of the faculties, but it is also a source of danger. By our vow we consecrate our heart to God and renounce the joys of family life. Yes, we do renounce the natural gift of God to women to become mothers for the greater gift, that of virgins of Christ, of becoming mothers of souls.

—————————DAY 266————

NOTHING CAN MAKE ME HOLY EXCEPT THE PRESence of God, and to me presence of God is fidelity to small things. . . . Nobody can live without food and water, and you must have that living conviction that you cannot live as a religious without feeding it with poverty, chastity, obedience, and wholehearted free service—and, above all, with prayer. You may say many prayers but to be able to pray you must be free, you must be clean, and you must be silent—that silence of the heart.

DAY 267

WE AVAIL OURSELVES OF EVERY OPPORTUNITY we can to proclaim his redeeming love, wherever we can find the spiritually poorest. Part of each day will be spent in the proclamation of the good news. We will deal not with crowds but with individuals, person to person, family to family, or, when necessary, with small groups where close contact is possible.

DAY 268

WE MUST BE CONVINCED THAT NOTHING ADORNS a human soul with greater splendor than the virtue of chastity, and nothing defiles a human soul more than the opposite vice. Yet there must be no mistake that the glory of chastity is not in immunity from temptation but in victory over these temptations.

DAY 269

THEN WE HAVE THE SILENCE OF THE EYES, which will always help us to see God. Our eyes are like two windows through which Christ or the world comes to our hearts. Often we need great courage to keep them closed. How often we say, "I wish I had not seen this thing," and yet we take so little trouble to overcome the desire to see everything.

DAY 270

WE MUST HAVE LOVE, KINDNESS, AND HEROISM that will touch the heart of God and so bring many a soul to the wounded heart of Christ. How pure our hands must be if we have to touch Christ's body as the priest touches him in the appearance of bread at the altar! With what love and devotion and faith he lifts the Sacred Host: the same we too must have when we lift the body of the sick poor. Let us put the same love, faith, and devotion into our action, and he will take it as done to him personally.

DAY 271

IF WE LOVE GOD WITH OUR WHOLE SOUL, IF WE have a love of Jesus Christ above all things, if we have a tender love for our Lady, we shall be less inclined to be unduly attached to creatures. In order that the love for Jesus may produce these effects, it must be intense, generous, and all-absorbing. It will so fill the mind and heart that we no longer give a thought to human affections. Should we unfortunately become entangled in any ill-ordered affections, Jesus, who cannot suffer strange gods in our hearts, will reproach us severely. He will himself protect with jealous care the hearts of those who give themselves to him.

DAY 272

TODAY, MORE THAN EVER, WE NEED TO PRAY FOR the light to know the will of God, for the love to accept the will of God, for the way to do the will of God.

DAY 273

THIS DOING OF THE WILL OF GOD IS OBEDIENCE. Jesus came to do the will of his Father and did it unto death, death on the cross. "Be it done to me according to your word" was our Lady's answer. For you and for me who have been chosen to be his own by becoming Missionaries of Charity, the surest way to true holiness and the fulfillment of our mission of love, peace, and joy is through obedience.

DAY 274

THIS MUST EXCITE IN US CONFIDENCE IN THE providence of God who preserves even the birds and the flowers. Surely if God feeds the young ravens, which cry to him, if he nourishes the birds, which neither sow nor reap nor gather into barns, if he vests the flowers of the field so beautifully, how much more will he care for men whom he has made in his own image and likeness and adopted as his children, if we only act as such, keep his commandments, and always entertain a filial confidence in him.

—DAY 275—

AS OUR SOCIETY KEEPS GROWING, NATURALLY there is a danger of that beautiful spirit of family diminishing, but it is for each one of us to protect it and make the life of love and unity, of humility and service, live and bring much fruit in each one of us and in the people we serve. The means to protect this family spirit of love and unity is spiritual life. We must be able to uplift each other and, through the good example of a life of prayer and union with God, encourage and help each other to remain faithful to our vocation.

—DAY 276—

TRULY HE HAS LOVED ME UNTO DEATH. DO I LOVE Jesus unto death? How can I love Jesus, whom I do not see, if I don't love my sister—our poor—whom I see? If I do not, Saint John said, "You are a liar."

—DAY 277—

THE BEAUTIFUL NAME *SISTER* IS ANOTHER STRONG tie of the members of the same family. The sacredness of it is so great that King Solomon, in his Song of Songs, calls the soul by this sweet name.

—DAY 278—

IN THE POOR, AND IN OUR SISTERS, IT IS JESUS, and so we are twenty-four hours in his presence. Therefore we are contemplatives in the heart of the world. If we would only learn how to pray the work by doing it with Jesus, for Jesus, to Jesus, for the glory of his name and the good of souls!

—DAY 279—

IF SOMETIMES WE FEEL AS IF THE MASTER IS away, is it not because I have kept myself far from some sister? One thing that will always secure heaven for us: acts of charity and kindness with which we have filled our lives. We will never know how much good just a simple smile can do. We tell people how kind, forgiving, and understanding God is. Are we the living proof? Can they really see this kindness, this forgiveness, this understanding, alive in us?

DAY 280

THERE ARE MANY WHO DO NOT KNOW, MANY who do not dare, and many who do not want to pray. In the communion of saints we act and pray in their names.

DAY 281

IF YOU DON'T HAVE LOVE FOR ONE ANOTHER, then how can you love people outside? How can they see Jesus in others? That's why we need a clean heart, to be able to see Jesus in each other. To love one another as Jesus has loved each one, that's all Jesus came to teach us. The whole gospel is very, very simple. Do you love me? Obey my commandments. He's turning and twisting just to get around to one thing: love one another. He wants us to be really, really loving. Give from the heart.

BE KIND IN YOUR ACTIONS. DO NOT THINK THAT you are the only one who can do efficient work, work worth showing. This makes you harsh in your judgment of the other sisters, who may not have the same talents. God will ask of that sister only what he has given her, and not what he has given you; so why interfere with the plan of God? All things are his, and he gives as he pleases. You do your best and think that others do their best for God's own purpose. Their best may be a total failure. What is that to you? You follow the way he has chosen for you. For others also, let him choose.

THE APOSTLES ASKED JESUS TO TEACH THEM TO pray . . . and he taught them the beautiful prayer, the Our Father . . . I believe each time we say the Our Father, God looks at his hand, where he has carved us—"I have carved you on the palm of my hand"—he looks at his hand, and he sees you there (Isaiah 49:16, paraphrased). How wonderful the tenderness and love of the great God!

THOUGHTFULNESS IS THE BEGINNING OF GREAT sanctity. If you learn this art of being thoughtful, you will become more and more Christlike, for his heart was meek and he always thought of others. Our vocation to be beautiful must be full of thought for others. Jesus "went about doing good." Our Lady did nothing else in Cana but thought of the need of the others and made their need known to Jesus. The thoughtfulness of Jesus and Mary and Joseph was so great that it made Nazareth the abode of God Most High. If we also have that kind of thoughtfulness for each other, our communities will really become the abode of God Most High.

HOW BEAUTIFUL OUR CONVENTS WILL BECOME where there is this total thoughtfulness of each other's needs! The quickest and the surest way is the tongue: use it for the good of others. If you think well of others, you will also speak well of others and to others. From the abundance of the heart the mouth speaks (Luke 6:45, paraphrased). If your heart is full of love, you will speak of love.

DAY 286

WE ARE INFALLIBLE WHEN WE OBEY. ASK THE Holy Spirit to give us that one grace. Only Jesus in the Blessed Sacrament, Jesus on the cross, can teach us obedience, and that is by the reality of his own example.

DAY 287

IN ONE WORD, BE A REAL BRANCH ON THE VINE, Jesus. . . . The surest means to this will be to deepen our love for each other: knowing each other's lovableness; feeling the need of each other; speaking well of each other and to each other; appreciating and knowing the gifts and abilities of each other.

DAY 288

"IF A MAN LOVE ME, HE WILL KEEP MY WORDS" (John 14:23 KJV). "My new commandment: Love one another as I have loved you" (John 13:34, paraphrased). "My Father will love him, and we will come to him and make our home with him" (John 14:23 RSV). In loving one another through our works we bring an increase of grace and a growth in divine love. Since Jesus' love is our mutual love, we will be able to love as he loves, and he will manifest himself through us to each other and to the world; by this mutual love they will know that we are his.

DAY 289

LOVE TO PRAY, FEEL THE NEED TO PRAY OFTEN during the day, and take the trouble to pray. If you want to pray better, you must pray more. Prayer enlarges the heart until it is capable of containing God's gift of himself. Ask and seek, and your heart will grow big enough to receive him and keep him as your own.

—DAY 290—

LOVE—REALLY BE A CONTEMPLATIVE IN THE heart of the world. Whatever you do, even if you help somebody cross the road, you do it to Jesus. Even giving somebody a glass of water, you do it to Jesus. It is simple, what you do in the community is very, very important, for love begins at home.

—DAY 291—

SAINT THÉRÈSE, THE LITTLE FLOWER, SAID: "When I act and think with charity, I feel it is Jesus who works within me. The closer I am united with him, the more I love all the other dwellers in Carmel." To understand this and practice it we need much prayer, which unites us with God and overflows continually upon others. Our works of charity are nothing but the overflow of our love for God from within. Therefore, the one who is most united to him loves her neighbor most.

DAY 292

THIS COMPLETE SURRENDER OF SELF TO GOD must secure for us perseverance in God's service, since by obedience we always do his most holy will and consequently obtain freedom from doubts, anxieties, and scruples.

DAY 293

LET US UNDERSTAND THE TENDERNESS OF GOD'S love. For he speaks in the Scripture, "Even if a mother could forget her child, I will not forget you. I have carved you on the palm of my hand" (Isaiah 49:15–16, paraphrased). When you feel lonely, when you feel unwanted, when you feel sick and forgotten, remember you are precious to him. He loves you. And show that love for one another, for this is all that Jesus came to teach us.

---DAY 294---

WE MUST BE SOULS OF PRAYER BECAUSE WE ARE
so exposed to the world. Jesus said, "They are in the world,
but not of the world!" (John 17:14, paraphrased). That is the
reason why it is most important for us to be deeply contemplative. "I no longer live, but Christ lives in me" (Galatians
2:20 NIV). This is the fruit of prayer: to allow him to live in
us and to use us without our counting the cost. We can do
that only if we are deeply in love with Jesus. When we speak
of contemplation, we think of the contemplatives, but in our
constitutions it is beautifully put: "We must be deeply contemplative." It means that deep oneness with him, to have
that clear vision so that he can use us as he wants.

---DAY 295---

INDIVIDUALS OF ANY NATIONALITY ARE WEL-
come in our Society because in this as in everything else
we want to be true children of our holy Mother Church.
Nationalism is inconsistent with our constitutions, and
renders us unfaithful to the spirit of our vocation. Hence
we should never fasten an unfavorable opinion on people

belonging to another nation than ours, for this would speak great want of charity.

---DAY 296---

SAINT CLEMENT RELATED HAVING HEARD FROM Saint Peter that our Lord was accustomed to watch like a mother with her children, near his disciples during their sleep to render them any little service. Such is the chain that unites and binds us, the old with the young, a chain of gold, a thousand times stronger than flesh and blood, interest or friendship, because these permit the defects of the body and the vices of the soul to be seen, while charity covers all, hides all, to offer exclusively to admiration and love the work of the hands of God, the price of the blood of Jesus Christ, and the masterpiece of the Holy Spirit.

---DAY 297---

WE MUST NOT BE AFRAID TO PROCLAIM CHRIST'S love and love as he loved. In the work we have to do—it does not matter how small or humble it may be—make it Christ's love in action. Do not be afraid to be poor and so proclaim his poverty. Be not afraid to keep a clean and undivided heart and so radiate the joy of being the spouse of Jesus crucified. Do not be afraid to go down with Christ and be subject to those who have authority from above and so declare Christ's obedience unto death. Rejoice that one more Christ is walking through the world in you and through you, going about doing good.

DAY 298

THE MOST IMPORTANT RULE OF A WELL-regulated family, of a family founded on love and unity, is that the children show an unbounded trust in and obedience to their parents. Jesus practiced this for thirty years in Nazareth, for we hear nothing of him but that he was subject to them, that is, he did what he was told.

DAY 299

UNITY IS THE FRUIT OF PRAYER, OF HUMILITY, OF love. Therefore, if the community prays together, it will stay together, and if you stay together, you will love one another as Jesus loves each one of you. A real change of heart will make it really one heart full of love. This one heart our community offers to Jesus and to our Lady, his mother.

DAY 300

I WANT YOU ALL TO FILL YOUR HEARTS WITH great love. Don't imagine that love, to be true and burning, must be extraordinary. No; what we need in our love is the continuity to love the One we love.

DAY 301

OBEDIENCE TRANSFORMS SMALL, COMMONPLACE things and occupations into acts of living faith, and faith in action is love, and love in action is service of the loving God. Obedience lived with joy creates a living awareness of the presence of God, so that fidelity to acts of obedience such as the bell, timetable, or the eating of food, which are the fruit of constant, prompt, cheerful, undivided obedience, become like drops of oil that keep the light of Jesus living in our life.

—DAY 302—

SOME INTERIOR AND EXTERIOR HELPS TO chastity:

Diffidence in ourselves and a very special confidence in God and the Sacred Heart of Jesus, who is the fountain and source of all sanctity.

The memory of the presence of God and the spirit of prayer.

Frequent reception of the Holy Eucharist, which is the wheat of the elect.

Mortification of the flesh.

Faithful observances of the rules of modesty and the rule of touch, and supreme contempt for particular friendship. True friendship is a gift of God. Real friendship is affectionate and reserved, is not exclusive, and allows freedom in the choice of friends.

The spirit of work, even in the hot season.

Straightforwardness with our superior and with our spiritual father in our confessions.

Great prudence, especially in dealing with the other sex. Imprudence has caused the ruin of many religious.

A personal love of our Lady, the virgin undefiled. She will watch over us and if we fail, let us remember that she is the refuge of sinners.

DAY 303

THE POOR PEOPLE ARE VERY GREAT PEOPLE. They can teach us so many beautiful things. The other day one of them came to thank us and said, "You people who have vowed chastity, you are the best people to teach us family planning because it is nothing more than self-control out of love for each other." And I think he said something beautiful. These are people who maybe have nothing to eat, maybe they have not a home where to live, but they are great people.

DAY 304

LET US BE VERY SINCERE IN OUR DEALINGS WITH each other and have the courage to accept one another as we are. Do not be surprised or become preoccupied at each other's failings; rather see and find in each other the good, for each one of us is created in the image of God. Jesus has said it so beautifully: "I am the vine, you are the branches, and my Father is the vinedresser" (John 15:1, 5, paraphrased). Let us try to see and accept that every sister is a branch in Christ the vine. The life-giving sap that flows from the vine (Jesus) through each of the branches (sisters) is the same.

—DAY 305—

A CERTAIN PRIEST LOVED THE CHINESE AND wanted to do something for them. He went completely into the work. Now if I live constantly in the company of Jesus, I too will do the same as he did. Nothing pleases God more than when we obey. Let us love God not for what he gives but for what he deigns to take from us: our little acts of obedience that give us the occasion of proving our love for him.

DAY 306

OFTEN OUR PRAYERS DO NOT PRODUCE RESULTS because we have not fixed our mind and heart on Christ, through whom our prayers can ascend to God. Often a deep, fervent look at Christ may make the most fervent prayer. "I look at him and he looks at me" is the most perfect prayer.

DAY 307

IN EVERY AGE GOD HAS PICKED SOMEBODY TO take care of the poor. Missionaries of Charity have a special part to play in the Church. That is why bad behavior with each other does not fit with our life. We are not only missionaries. We have been sent to be "witnesses of his love and compassion." As missionaries we must be . . . ever ready to go to any part of the world anytime, respect and appreciate unfamiliar customs of other peoples, their living conditions and language, willing to adapt ourselves if and when necessary, and happy to undertake any labor and toil, and glad to make any sacrifice involved in our missionary life.

DAY 308

WHAT IS NOT HUMILITY:

Moodiness when humiliated, when corrected. Trying always to excuse oneself.

Refusing to acknowledge one's fault, even being dishonest with oneself.

Putting the blame on somebody.

Ambitious to acquire praise.

Yearning to be in charge of everything, to control all.

DAY 309

OUR TOTAL SURRENDER WILL COME TODAY BY surrendering even our sins so that we will be poor. "Unless you become a child you cannot come to me." You are too big, too heavy; you cannot be lifted up. We need humility to acknowledge our sin. The knowledge of our sin helps us to rise. "I will get up and go to my father" (Luke 15:18 NASB).

—DAY 310—

CHEERFULNESS IS INDEED THE FRUIT OF THE Holy Spirit and a clear sign of the kingdom within. Jesus shared his joy with his disciples: "That my joy may be in you, and that your joy may be full" (John 15:11 RSV). Our joy is a sign of our generosity, selflessness, and close union with God; for he gives most who gives with joy, and "God loves a cheerful giver" (2 Corinthians 9:7 ESV).

—DAY 311—

WE SHALL GO FREELY IN THE NAME OF JESUS, TO towns and villages all over the world, even amid squalid and dangerous surroundings, with Mary the Immaculate Mother of Jesus, seeking out the spiritually poorest of the poor with God's own tender affection and proclaiming to them the good news of salvation and hope, singing with them his songs, bringing to them his love, peace, and joy.

—DAY 312—

WE ALSO MUST UNDERSTAND THAT WE ARE SIN-
ners and that we need confession. And also we must
experience that mercy of God to be able to radiate that
joy, because that is what has destroyed much of the joy
and faith in the Church today, because people have lost
that need, that use for confession. That is why there is
so much unrest. . . . The loss of the use of confession has
brought much mental suffering because you must remove
that thing, that sin. I can get rid of sin, I can be free of
sin, because I believe that the mercy of God is greater than
any sin.

—DAY 313—

WHEN YOUNG PEOPLE COME TO VISIT US, I TEACH
them to love each other. Jesus said, "Love one another as
I have loved you" (John 15:12, paraphrased). Very often
young men come to us to work with the lepers. I teach
them how to love each other and how to see God through
this kind of love. If you come to India, I will teach you

too. Love in action is the most dear to me. For this kind of love, we draw strength from prayer. This is real love and we give our lives for this kind of action. It is not possible to show God's love for people without being in loving service to others.

<hr>—— DAY 314 ——<hr>

EVERYBODY NOW KNOWS THE POOR. BEFORE, people could not believe that people were dying, that they were really poor and so on. Now, through the work, many people have come into close contact with the dying, with the lepers, with the sick, with the poor, with the unwanted. And this awareness and this concern is creating more and more people to do something, to put their love in a living action. The congregation of the Missionaries of Charity is just a little instrument in the hands of God. We must try to keep it always like that—the small instrument. Very often I feel like a little pencil in God's hand. He does the writing, he does the thinking, he does the movement—I have only to be a pencil and nothing else.

A RICH MAN OF DELHI, IN SPEAKING OF OUR Society, said, "How wonderful it is to see sisters so free from the world—in the twentieth century, when one thinks everything is old-fashioned but the present day." Keep to the simple ways of poverty: of repairing your shoes, and so on—of loving poverty as you love your mother.

HUMILITY IS TRUTH; THEREFORE, IN ALL SINCER-ity we must be able to look up and say, "I can do all things in him who strengthens me" (Philippians 4:13 RSV). Because of this assertion of Saint Paul, you must have a certain confidence in doing your work—or rather God's work—well, efficiently, even perfectly with Jesus and for Jesus. Be also convinced that you by yourself can do nothing, that you have nothing but sin, weakness, and misery. All the gifts of nature and of grace that you have, you have them from God.

——— DAY 317———

OUR CHILDREN, WE WANT THEM, WE LOVE THEM; but what of the other millions? Many people are very, very concerned with the children of India, with the children of Africa, where quite a number die of malnutrition, of hunger, and so on. But millions of others are dying deliberately by the will of their own mothers. And this is what is the greatest destroyer of peace today. Because if a mother can kill her own child, what is left before I kill you and you kill me? There is nothing in between.

——— DAY 318———

OUR CONSTITUTIONS ARE VERY CLEAR; WE MUST make our community deeply contemplative, intensely eucharistic, and vibrant with joy. Do we know the meaning of being "deeply contemplative"? Am I so attached to Jesus? Do I have that personal attachment to Jesus? "Deeply contemplative," you have chosen to be a contemplative, that deep silence should be in the house. The way we pray, the way we talk, the way we walk, that tender love for each other, all that's the fruit of contemplation.

177

DAY 319

WHAT DOES IT MEAN TO BE A CONTEMPLATIVE?
It means one who is intimately and personally attached to
Jesus. It means to allow Jesus to live his life in you. If you
are truly deeply contemplative, if you have the desire for
that personal attachment to Jesus, then it is beautiful.

DAY 320

LET US ASK OUR LADY AND SAINT JOSEPH TO
make our communities what they made Nazareth for
Jesus. Let us not be afraid. Jesus said, "Do not be afraid—I
am with you!" (Isaiah 41:10 GNT) and "Love one another,
as I have loved you" (John 13:34–35 DRA). By this they
will know that you belong to Jesus. Love does not live on
words, nor can it be explained by words. Above all, that
love, which is in him and comes from him and which
finds him, touches him, and serves him, loves him in
others. Such love is true, burning, pure, without fear and
doubt. No greater love than the love Christ himself has
shown us. So I ask you to love one another as he has
loved us. As the Father has loved him, he has loved us,

and loves us now. He has called us by our name; we are precious to him.

————————DAY 321————————

THROUGH THE HOLY SPIRIT, THE SPIRIT OF LOVE, the spirit of purity, through the spirit of deep faith, we can persevere. You will feel lonely, helpless, and hopeless. But remember: he wants you to be here, believe! You don't have to go around for now and preach. Your presence is enough! Saint Francis one day took a brother and told him, "Let us go and preach." He walked for a few hours praying in silence. And when the brother asked him, "When will we start preaching?" Francis answered, "We had done the best preaching by our silence, presence, and prayer."

————————DAY 322————————

SISTERS, BE ALWAYS RECOLLECTED, BE ALWAYS cheerful. Smile! Radiate the presence of Jesus through your joy. Your apostolate is to smile and pray. Put love in whatever you do. The smaller the things, the greater the love. It is not how much you do but how much love you are putting in what you do. And remember you do it to Jesus. Jesus said: "I was hungry and you gave me to eat, I was sick and you visited me, I was lonely and you took care of me. . . . *You did it to me*!"

DAY 323

WE DO WITH JESUS, THROUGH JESUS, TO JESUS. Why do we always connect contemplation with action? Jesus said, "I was hungry . . . I was naked . . ." It is something sacred, sisters, but it cannot grow unless you live it. Whatever work you do by obedience you are doing it to Jesus; in the convent also you fulfill your vow . . . as every sister is the poorest of the poor. Now, by talking to you from my heart, [I am] fulfilling my fourth vow. How do I love Jesus in action? By my wholehearted service, in the freedom of poverty and the surrender of obedience. To do all these four things I must be a soul of prayer and have a deep prayer life.

WHAT IS THE CONTEMPLATIVE LIFE TO YOU? IS it just a number of hours of adoration, extra prayer, fasting, or penance? That extra prayer doesn't make you a contemplative, sisters. These are means. It's what happens inside and that matters. God speaks in our interior, in our heart. He speaks in silence. Hear him speak in your heart. As Saint Paul said, "I live now not I, but Christ lives in me" (Galatians 2:20, paraphrased). He loves in me.

SOULS OF PRAYER ARE SOULS OF GREAT SILENCE. In the Eucharist his silence is the highest, the truest praise of the Father. As contemplatives you are to simply be the sign of Divine Presence. Sisters, you need silence to be alone with God. It is the root of your union with God and with one another. Without it you will lose your vocation, and your whole life as Missionaries of Charity. Contemplative life will collapse. Sisters, help each other to keep that deep silence and recollection. Sisters, you must take the means to keep silence.

DAY 326

JOY IS A NEED AND A POWER FOR US, EVEN PHYS-
ically. A sister who has cultivated a spirit of joy feels less
tired and is always ready to go doing good. A sister filled
with joy preaches without preaching. A joyful sister is like
the sunshine of God's love, the hope of eternal happiness,
the flame of burning love.

DAY 327

WE NEED PRAYER. IT IS LIKE A CAR THAT NEEDS
refilling every day. That is why we need Holy Communion,
we need prayers, we need penance, we need meditation, to
be able to be refilled. Like the car cannot move without
petrol, we cannot continue without prayer in our life.

DAY 328

FACE YOURSELF WITH A PURE HEART. FOR A
pure heart can see God. See him in your own heart first.
Don't pretend. Be sincere. Purity begins in your heart.

Then you will see Jesus in the distressing disguise twenty-four hours. Seeing and touching Christ twenty-four hours, this is contemplation. Contemplative life can be a very easy life. Unless your heart is free, unless it is pure, you will not see Jesus, and you will not be able to love.

DAY 329

LET US BEG FROM OUR LADY TO MAKE OUR hearts "meek and humble" like her Son's was. It was from her and in her that the heart of Jesus was formed.

DAY 330

WE NEED YOU TO BE REALLY CONTEMPLATIVES, really souls of prayer. If you put your whole heart into your prayer, if you make every effort to be simple and obedient, then you will become holy. Humility and obedience are a sure way to holiness. And don't let any type of uncharitableness touch you. Get rid of it immediately. Then you will be true spouses of Jesus crucified.

—DAY 331—

THE ACTIVE SISTERS HAVE TO GIVE JESUS BY taking care of the people, feeding them, clothing them, and so on. You must give Jesus to the people by really living a life of deep prayer, penance, and mortification, that deep attachment to Jesus. Take the trouble to really determine to be holy.

—DAY 332—

AS MISSIONARIES WE MUST BE . . . READY TO accept joyously to die daily if we want to bring souls to God—to pay the price he paid for souls . . . happy to undertake any labor and toil, and glad to make any sacrifice involved in our missionary life.

—DAY 333—

IN THE CHAPEL I WANT YOU TO SHOW THAT DEEP, deep reverence. The Holy Father—the whole Church—is busy to show love, to show respect for the Blessed

Sacrament. Take trouble to genuflect and do it deliberately. That is an act of adoration. If you are united to Jesus, this will come naturally—no need to force yourself. . . . When you genuflect, remain there on the floor for a second; genuflect because life is there.

—————————DAY 334—————————

SISTERS, WHEN YOU ARE OUT VISITING THE people, do it with your whole heart and soul. . . . It may be a first and last time for somebody to obtain that grace. Maybe God can speak to that particular soul only through you; he can touch that person only through you. Your presence will radiate his touch. You are touching the soul with the Word of God.

—————————DAY 335—————————

PRAYER IS THE FRUIT OF SACRIFICE. IF YOU ARE in love with him, he will bring many souls to himself through you. You may never know them, but he will do it.

DAY 336

THE SILENCE OF THE MIND AND OF THE HEART: and our Lady "kept all these words in her heart" (Luke 2:51 DRA). This silence brought her close to God—she never had to regret anything. See what she did when Saint Joseph was troubled. One word from her would have cleared his mind; she did not say that word, and our Lord himself worked the miracle to clear her name. Would that we could be so convinced of this necessity of silence! I think then the road to close union with God will become very clear.

DAY 337

LET US THANK GOD FOR ALL HIS LOVE FOR US, IN so many ways and in so many places. Let us in return, as an act of gratitude and adoration, determine to be holy because he is holy. Each time Jesus wanted to prove his love for us, he was rejected by mankind. Before his birth, his parents asked for a simple dwelling place and there was none.

---DAY 338---

SEE HOW OUR LADY OBEYED THE ANGEL: "BE IT done to me according to thy word" (Luke 1:38, paraphrased). Whose word? The angel's, because he took the place of God. He was sent by God to her. She, the queen of heaven, obeys the angel. See how she obeyed Saint Joseph, with what love and submission, without an excuse. To her, Saint Joseph was "he" whose place he took.

---DAY 339---

CHEERFULNESS AND JOY WERE OUR LADY'S strength. This made her a willing handmaid of God, her Son, for as soon as he came to her she "went in haste." Only joy could have given her the strength to go in haste over the hills of Judea to do the work of handmaid to her cousin. So with us too; we like her must be true handmaids of the Lord and daily after Holy Communion go in haste, over the hills of difficulties we meet in giving wholehearted service to the poor. Give Jesus to the poor as the handmaid of the Lord.

IT IS THAT TOTAL SURRENDER TO GOD THAT makes me a religious. Again, we come back to our Lord and our Lady: I am sent by my Father; "my Father is greater than I" (John 14:28 KJV). Jesus need not have done all that he did. He is equal to God: God from God, Light from Light, and yet he submitted: to obey, to be born, to go down to Nazareth. He accepted to be put here and there. When the high priest asked him, "Tell us whether you be the Christ," Jesus obeyed and gave the answer. He knew that if he obeyed it would be crucifixion, but he was totally surrendered. Have we come here to be equal? We have come here to be totally surrendered.

IF YOU ARE HUMBLE, NOTHING WILL TOUCH YOU, neither praise nor disgrace, because you know what you are. If you are blamed, you won't be discouraged; if anyone calls you a saint, you won't put yourself on a pedestal. If you are a saint, thank God; if you are a sinner, don't remain one. Christ tells us to aim very high, not to be like

Abraham or David or any of the saints, but to be like our heavenly Father.

DAY 342

THE SEASON OF ADVENT IS LIKE SPRINGTIME IN nature, when everything is renewed and so is fresh and healthy. Advent is also meant to do this to us—to refresh us and make us healthy, to be able to receive Christ in whatever form he may come to us. At Christmas he comes like a little child, so small, so helpless, so much in need of his mother and all that a mother's love can give. It was his mother's humility that enabled her to receive Jesus as a helpless babe, her humility that helped her to do the works of handmaid to Christ—God of God, true God of true God, being of one substance with the Father by whom all things were made. Let us see and touch the greatness that fills the depths of their humility. We cannot do better than Jesus and Mary. If we really want God to fill us, we must empty ourselves through humility of all that is selfishness in us.

LET US BEG FROM OUR LADY TO MAKE OUR hearts "meek and humble" as her Son's was. It was from her and in her that the heart of Jesus was formed. Let us all try during this month to pray for this again and again and practice humility and meekness. We learn humility through accepting humiliations cheerfully. Do not let a chance pass you by. It is so very easy to be proud, harsh, moody, and selfish—so easy. But we have been created for greater things; why stoop down to things that will spoil the beauty of our hearts?

HUMILITY ALWAYS RADIATES THE GREATNESS and glory of God. How wonderful are the ways of God! He used humility, smallness, helplessness, and poverty to prove to the world that he loved the world. Let the Missionaries of Charity not be afraid to be humble, small, and helpless to prove their love to God.

DAY 345

ONCE THE LONGING FOR MONEY COMES, THE longing also comes for what money can give; superfluities, nice rooms, luxuries at table, more clothes, fans, and so on. Our needs will increase, for one thing brings another, and the result will be endless dissatisfaction. This is how it comes. If you ever happen to have to get things, remember that the superiors have to depend on you. As a religious you must buy things of cheaper quality, and your good example in saving will keep up the spirit of poverty.

DAY 346

LET US REALLY TAKE THE TROUBLE TO LEARN the lesson of holiness from Jesus, whose heart was meek and humble. The first lesson from this heart is our examination of conscience . . . and the rest and love and service follow at once. Examination is not our work alone, but a partnership between us and Jesus. We should not rest in a useless look at our own miseries but should lift our hearts to God and in his light see ourselves. If we are sincere, we will let his light enlighten us and make him to have his way with us.

191

DAY 347

"THE KINGDOM OF HEAVEN IS LIKE TO A MER-chant seeking good pearls" (Matthew 13:45 DRA). Yes, we have promised great things but greater things are promised us. Be faithful to Christ and pray for perseverance. Remember to say to yourself, "I have been created for greater things." Never stoop lower than the ideal. Let nothing satisfy you but God.

DAY 348

YOU MAY HAVE VISIONS AND ECSTASIES AND YET be deceived. Watch! There are the silk threads of pride and deception; for example, hiding good qualities: a good voice, the ability to make others happy, and so on. "I cannot do this. I cannot do that, but I can be lazy." Pride is often covered by laziness.

DAY 349

COMPLAINING AND EXCUSING ONESELF ARE MOST natural, but they are a means the devil makes use of to increase our pride. Correction at times hurts most when it is most true.

DAY 350

HUMILITY IS THE MOTHER OF ALL VIRTUES: purity, charity, obedience. Saint Bernard and all the saints built their lives on humility. Charitableness and pride cannot go together because pride is all for self, and charity wants to give. The sisters most liked are those who are humble. Self-knowledge puts us on our knees, and it is very necessary for love. For knowledge of God gives love, and knowledge of self gives humility.

—DAY 351—

LOVE JESUS WITH A BIG HEART. SERVE JESUS with joy and gladness of spirit, casting aside and forgetting all that troubles and worries you. To be able to do all these, pray lovingly like children, with an earnest desire to love much and make loved the love that is not loved.

—DAY 352—

THESE ARE THE FEW WAYS WE CAN PRACTICE humility:

To speak as little as possible of oneself.

To mind one's own business.

Not to want to manage other people's affairs.

To avoid curiosity.

To accept contradiction and correction cheerfully. To pass over the mistakes of others.

To accept insults and injuries.

To accept being slighted, forgotten, and disliked. Not to seek to be specially loved and admired.

To be kind and gentle even under provocation. Never to stand on one's dignity.

To yield in discussion even though one is right. To choose always the hardest.

TO EXPRESS OUR UNION AND SHARING IN THE sufferings of our poor for their salvation and sanctification, we seek all opportunities of self-forgetfulness, giving ourselves with devotion and love to the least of our brethren, disregarding all fatigue, ingratitude, apparent uselessness, disappointments, frustrations, failures, humiliations involved in our service of love.

JOY IS NOT SIMPLY A MATTER OF TEMPERAMENT in the service of God and souls; it is always hard. All the more reason why we should try to acquire it and make it grow in our hearts.

DAY 355

THE MISSIONARY COMES FOR A PURPOSE. GOD SO loved the world that he sent his only Son. Just as Jesus was sent, we too! . . . We have been sent with a purpose: to be his love.

DAY 356

WE DESIRE TO BE ABLE TO WELCOME JESUS AT Christmastime, not in a cold manger of our heart, but in a heart full of love and humility, in a heart so pure, so immaculate, so warm with love for one another.

DAY 357

THE HUMILITY OF JESUS CAN BE SEEN IN THE crib, in the exile of Egypt, in the hidden life, in the inability to make people understand him, in the desertion of his apostles, in the hatred of his persecutors in all the terrible suffering and death of his Passion, and now in his permanent state of humility in the tabernacle, where he has reduced himself to such a small particle of bread that the priest can hold him with two fingers. The more we empty ourselves, the more room we give God to fill us.

DAY 358

JESUS CAME INTO THIS WORLD FOR ONE PURpose. He came to give us the good news that God loves us, that God is love, that he loves you, and he loves me. He wants us to love one another as he loves each one of us. Let us love him. How did the Father love him? He gave him to us. How did Jesus love you and me? By giving his life. He gave all that he had—his life—for you and me. He died on the cross because he loved us, and he wants us to love one another as he loves each one of us. When we look at the cross, we know how he loved us. When we look at the tabernacle, we know how he loves us now, you and me, your family, and everybody's family with a tender love. And God loves us with a tender love. That is all that Jesus came to teach us, the tender love of God. "I have called you by your name, you are mine" (Isaiah 43:1, paraphrased).

197

—DAY 359—

MAY THE JOY OF THE RISEN JESUS CHRIST BE with you, to bring joy into your very soul. The good God has given himself to us. In Bethlehem, joy filled the cave. "I bring you good tidings of great joy," said the angel (Luke 2:10 KJV). In his life, Jesus wanted to share his joy with his apostles: "That my joy may be in you" (John 15:11 RSV). Joy was the password of the first Christians. Saint Paul, how often he repeated himself: "Rejoice in the Lord always; again I will say, Rejoice" (Philippians 4:4 RSV). In return for the great grace of baptism, the priest tells the newly baptized, "May you serve the church joyfully."

—DAY 360—

THE COMING OF JESUS AT BETHLEHEM BROUGHT joy to the world and to every human heart. The same Jesus comes again and again in our hearts during Holy Communion. He wants to give the same joy and peace. May his coming this Christmas bring to each one of us that peace and joy that he desires to give. Let us pray much for this grace of peace and joy in our own heart, in our communities, in our Society, and in the Church.

---DAY 361---

TODAY LET US RECALL THE LOVE OF GOD FOR you and for me. His love is so tender. His love is so great, so real, so living that Jesus came just to teach us that— how to love. And love is not something that passes, but something that lives. Works of love, and this living love is the way to peace. And where does this love begin? Right in our hearts. We must know that we have been created for greater things, not just to be a number in the world, not just to go for diplomas and degrees and this work and that work. We have been created with a purpose, to love and to be loved.

---DAY 362---

WE HAVE ALL TRIED IN SOME WAY OR ANOTHER to be a real joy to our Lady. So often during the day, we call her the "cause of our joy" and the joy of her Son is our strength. . . . Let us promise that we will make our community another Bethlehem, another Nazareth. Let us love each other as we love Jesus. In Nazareth there was love, unity, prayer, sacrifice, and hard work; and there was especially a deep understanding and appreciation of each other and thoughtfulness for each other.

—DAY 363—

BECAUSE GOD LOVES THE WORLD, HE SENT HIS Son. Now he sends you to be his Word, and that Word has to take flesh in the hearts of the people. That's why you need our Lady; when the Word of God came to her, became flesh in her, then she gave it to others. It is the same for you. The Word of God has come to you and has become flesh in you and then you must be able to give that love.

—DAY 364—

"WHO DO YOU SAY THAT I AM?" (MATTHEW 16:15 RSV).
You are God.
You are God from God.

You are begotten not made.

You are one in substance with the Father.

You are the Son of the living God.

You are the second person of the blessed Trinity. You are one with the Father.

You are in the Father from the beginning.

All things were made by you and the Father. You are the beloved Son in whom the Father is well pleased.

You are the son of Mary, conceived by the Holy Spirit in the womb of Mary.

You were born in Bethlehem.

You were wrapped in swaddling clothes by Mary and put in a manger full of straw.

You were kept warm by the breath of the donkey who carried your mother with you in her womb.

You are the son of Joseph the carpenter,
as known by the people of Nazareth.

You are an ordinary man without much learning,
as judged by the learned people of Israel.

TO ME—

Jesus is my God.

Jesus is my spouse.

Jesus is my life.

Jesus is my only love.

Jesus is my all in all.

Jesus is my everything.

Jesus, I love with my whole heart, with my whole being.

I have given him all, even my sins, and he has espoused me to himself in all tenderness and love.

Now and for life I am the spouse of my crucified Spouse.

Amen.

LIFE AND MINISTRY OF
MOTHER TERESA

GONXHA AGNES BOJAXHIU, FUTURE MOTHER
Teresa of Calcutta, was born on August 26, 1910, in Skopje
(in present-day North Macedonia), to Nikola and Drana
Bojaxhiu, fervent Catholics of Albanian descent. The
youngest of five children, two of whom died in infancy,
Gonxha grew up with her sister, Age, and her brother,
Lazar. Nikola was a prosperous merchant and passionate
patriot; Drana was the heart of the serene and welcom-
ing Bojaxhiu home. When Gonxha was nine years old,
her father died, by what was commonly assumed to have
been poisoning due to his involvement in the Albanian
national cause. This hard blow left the Bojaxhiu family in
a difficult financial situation. Yet the resourceful young
widow was able to meet the material needs of her family
and impart to her children the deeply religious values that
she herself possessed in abundance.

In addition to the firm Catholic upbringing she
received at home, Gonxha benefited greatly from her

participation in the parish community of the Sacred Heart, directed by the Jesuits. Strongly influenced by these fervent priests, the enthusiastic young girl grew in love for God and zeal for her faith. When she was only twelve years old, she first felt the call to be a missionary. Her vocation matured until at age eighteen she decided to join a missionary order of nuns. On September 26, 1928, she left home to join the Irish branch of the Institute of the Blessed Virgin Mary, commonly known as the Loreto Sisters.

Upon entering religious life, Gonxha received the name of Sister Teresa. She spent about two months in Dublin, then journeyed to India, arriving in Calcutta on January 6, 1929. After two years of novitiate in Darjeeling, Sister Teresa made her first profession of vows in May 1931 and was assigned to the Loreto Entally community in Calcutta. There she would spend more than seventeen years of her life as a teacher, and later principal, of St. Mary's School, winning the affection and admiration of both students and fellow sisters.

In May 1937 Sister Teresa made her final profession of vows and became a full-fledged member of the Loreto order. Known as prayerful, thoughtful, joyful, and hardworking, Mother Teresa found great happiness and fulfillment in her vocation as a Loreto nun. Amid her daily activities, her spiritual life would reach remarkable depths.

After nearly twenty years of life in Loreto, on September 10, 1946, while on the train to Darjeeling for her annual retreat, Mother Teresa received a new vocation—a "call within a call"—to found a religious congregation dedicated to the service of the poorest of the poor. After almost two years of discernment, in August 1948, with permission of her superiors, she left Loreto and began a new way of life in the slums of Calcutta.

Mother Teresa's first followers were her former students from St. Mary's school. She had already made a strong impact on them as their teacher, and now, in this new life of gospel service to the neediest that she exemplified, they saw an ideal worth leaving everything to follow. With eleven young women and Mother Teresa, the new missionary congregation, the Missionaries of Charity, was officially established in 1950 in Calcutta.

Clad in traditional Indian sari, the sisters of the new congregation were noted for their radical lifestyle and zeal. The joy they radiated in the streets and slums brought the light of God's love into the lives of the poorest of the poor. The attractive force of the little group drew other young women to join them and so the community grew rapidly. By 1960 they numbered more than a hundred, and their apostolic outreach increased; more slum schools, catechetical programs, homes for the dying, orphanages for abandoned children, medical dispensaries, and leprosy clinics were begun.

In 1965, after receiving pontifical recognition, Mother Teresa opened her first house outside India, in Cocorote, Venezuela. By the end of 1970, there were 30 houses in various cities and towns in India and 11 houses outside India. This was just the beginning of an astonishing worldwide expansion. Only a decade later, there were more than a thousand sisters in more than 180 houses in thirty countries on all five continents.

Wherever there was any need, in large cities or in small towns, in places beset by natural disasters or stricken by poverty, Mother Teresa and her Missionaries of Charity would seek out the poorest of the poor, the unloved and unwanted, the abandoned and rejected, offering them immediate and effective help. By "putting their love for God into a living action," they endeavored to restore to each person the dignity of a child of God, "created to love and be loved."

From the beginning of her new mission, many felt drawn to share in her "works of love" and so by 1963 an international association of "Co-Workers" came into being. Her religious family expanded to include other branches: the active brothers (1963), the contemplative sisters (1976), the contemplative brothers (1979), and the Fathers (1984).

Increasing admiration of Mother Teresa's new apostolate, in India and abroad, brought with it formal recognition of her accomplishments. In 1962 the Indian government awarded her the prestigious Padma Shri Award (Order of the Lotus). Mother Teresa accepted this award, as she did all future ones, with gratitude and appreciation, but remained unmoved by the honor received.

Two weeks later Mother Teresa traveled to Manila to receive the Magsaysay Award, her first on the international stage. Numerous awards and honors followed, among them the British Templeton Prize for Progress in Religion, the Soviet Peace Committee Prize, the US Presidential Medal of Freedom, Britain's Order of Merit, India's Bharat Ratna, the Catholic Church's John XXIII Award for Peace presented by Pope Paul VI, and in 1979 the prestigious Nobel Peace Prize.

An interview with Malcolm Muggeridge for BBC television in 1968 and his subsequent documentary and book *Something Beautiful for God* were instrumental in making Mother Teresa known in the Western world.

Within a decade she would become one of the most widely recognized and internationally acclaimed figures of the twentieth century, a veritable symbol of peace and sacrificial love, transcending political, social, religious, and geographic boundaries. Consequently, Mother Teresa became a highly sought-after speaker. She was invited to address the most varied audiences around the world, from village school children to the United Nations and the World Synod of Catholic Bishops. Her profound and simple sayings were treasured and repeated by people of all walks of life.

Through these years of increasing fame, Mother Teresa preserved a singularly attractive spirit of simplicity and authenticity. She considered herself unimportant, constantly emphasizing that all she and her followers did was "God's work." She always took every opportunity to draw attention to the poor, those whom she called "her people," to remind the world of their presence and of their dignity: "Our poor are great people."

But Mother Teresa was not just a representative of the poor. By embracing a lifestyle so similar to that of the people she served, she became one with them. Quick in action when her help was needed, she was there to salve wounds, to give a helping hand, to speak a word of comfort . . . to be a "mother." She never hesitated to roll up her sleeves and take part in the simplest household tasks, to spend time doing "little things" with "little people." Most importantly, she never lost sight of the presence and importance of the individual person, even when facing a crowd.

Always keeping the spiritual aspect of her work foremost in mind, she used to insist, "I think that we are not really social workers, but that we are really contemplatives right in the heart of the world." It was "to Christ in his distressing disguise of the poorest of the poor" that she ministered with so much "respect and love and devotion." Her conviction was based on the twenty-fifth chapter of Saint Matthew's gospel, as she tirelessly repeated in her speeches: "Jesus said, 'I was hungry, I was naked. I was sick. You did it to me.'" Thus, her daily living was the embodiment of her vision of faith. From God, in the silence and intimacy of prayer, she drew the strength to carry out her mission.

During the last decade of her life, Mother Teresa's health steadily declined. On September 5, 1997, at the age of eighty-seven, Mother Teresa went to her heavenly reward at the Mother House of the Missionaries of Charity in Calcutta, where she was buried after a state funeral.

In view of Mother Teresa's widespread reputation of holiness and the favors being reported, Pope John Paul II exceptionally permitted the opening of her Cause of Canonization before the normal waiting period of five years. She was beatified on October 19, 2003, by John Paul II and canonized by Pope Francis on September 4, 2016, both in Saint Peter's Square.

From the Publisher

GREAT BOOKS

ARE EVEN BETTER WHEN THEY'RE SHARED!

Help other readers find this one:

- Post a review at your favorite online bookseller

- Post a picture on a social media account and share why you enjoyed it

- Send a note to a friend who would also love it—or better yet, give them a copy

Thanks for reading!